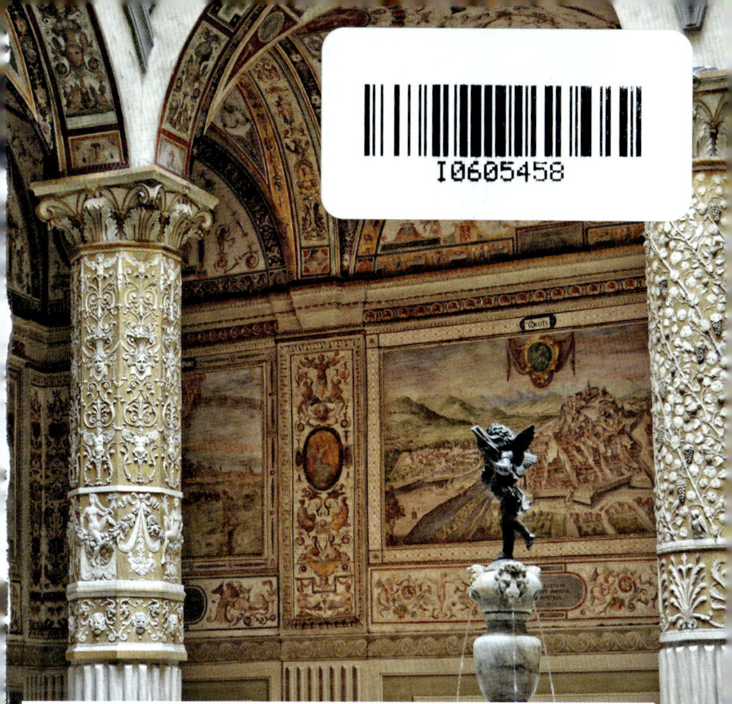

The **Mini Rough Guide** to

FLORENCE

YOUR TAILOR-MADE TRIP STARTS HERE

Tailor-made trips and unique adventures crafted by local experts

HOW ROUGHGUIDES.COM/TRIPS WORKS

STEP 1

Pick your dream destination, tell us what you want and submit an enquiry.

STEP 2

Fill in a short form to tell your local expert about your dream trip and preferences.

STEP 3

Our local expert will craft your tailor-made itinerary. You'll be able to tweak and refine it until you're completely satisfied.

STEP 4

Book online with ease, pack your bags and enjoy the trip! Our local expert will be on hand 24/7 while you're on the road.

PLAN AND BOOK YOUR TRIP AT
ROUGHGUIDES.COM/TRIPS

How to download your Free eBook

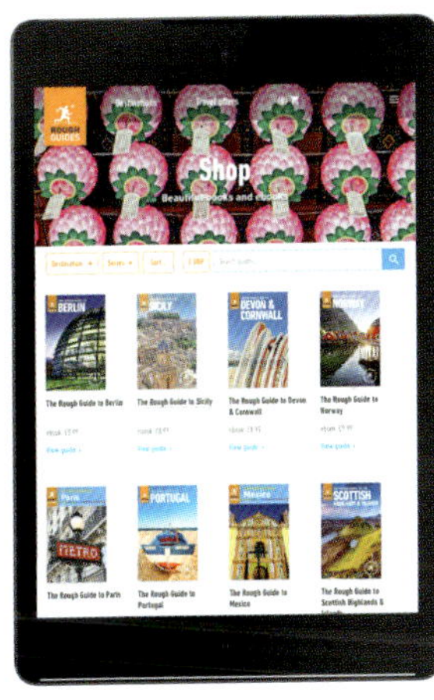

1. Visit **www.roughguides.com/free-ebook** or scan the **QR code** opposite

2. Enter the code **florence931**

3. Follow the simple step-by-step instructions

For troubleshooting contact: mail@roughguides.com

Contents

Introduction

The magnificent view from the hilltop church of San Miniato has changed little since the 16th century. The belvedere here looks out across the bridge-trellised Arno to Florence's *centro storico* (historic centre). It is a sea of terracotta rooftops interrupted only by the cupola (dome) of San Lorenzo, the medieval bell-tower of the Palazzo Vecchio and the focal point; the massive cupola of the Duomo.

The awesome contribution that Florence made to Western civilisation and culture was greatly out of proportion to its then diminutive size. Few nations, let alone cities, can boast of having nurtured such

WHAT'S NEW

Some of Florence's most treasured sites are newly sparkling thanks to restoration works. In 2024, the Brancacci Chapel reopened after years of meticulous labour, reviving Masaccio's brilliant frescoes which helped to ignite the spark of the Renaissance. Other renewals have included the Orsanmichele's trove of sculptures, Palazzo Pitti's Museum of Costume and Fashion and the Ponte Vecchio's Vasari Corridor.

Still under renovations are Santa Croce's Bardi Chapel and the Boboli Gardens' Porcelain Museum. Work on the Nuovi Uffizi is slated for final completion in 2026 following long term restoration and modernisation efforts – until then, Italy's most visited gallery remains open (in fresh, expanded form). Restorations of the famous Baptistery's vault, begun in 2022, are scheduled to end in 2028. In the meantime, its doors remain open while its floor-to-ceiling scaffolding offers visitors an unprecedented, face-to-face glimpse of its mosaics.

Look out too for a new Florence landmark, soon to be unveiled in the Santa Maria Novella complex: the National Museum of Italian ("MUNDI" for short), to showcase the history of the language from ancient origins and evolution through to the digital age, honouring Florentine movers and shakers like Dante and Boccaccio.

Viewpoint overlooking Brunelleschi's Dome

a remarkable heritage of artistic, literary, scientific and political talent in such a short period of time. Florence was, as D.H. Lawrence put it, 'man's perfect universe'. The roll call of artists and writers is an unparalleled record for any city; and remarkable for one whose uncontested period of greatness spanned less than 300 years.

Travel guides often compare Renaissance Florence with Athens in the 5th century BC, but while that glory is recalled only by spectacular ruins, Renaissance Florence remains intact and in evidence at every turn. Its historic palaces, great churches, exquisite sculptures and countless masterpieces are not crumbling relics, but a vivid and functional part of everyday life – worked in, lived in, prayed in, prized by present-day Florentines and open to all.

The elegant Palazzo Vecchio, where the first civic authority sat in the Middle Ages, still houses the offices of the city council.

Congregations kneel for mass in churches commissioned by medieval guilds. The jewellery stores lining the Ponte Vecchio are occupied by the descendants of goldsmiths who set up workshops here in the 14th century. Most of the city's narrow, cobbled side streets were wide enough to permit the passage of horse-drawn carts of centuries ago.

Not surprisingly, the city has proved irresistible to tourists since the late 18th century, when Florence and its treasures became an unmissable stop on the 'Grand Tour' undertaken by the British gentry. Today, the medieval alleys are lined with ice cream bars and pizzerias. Postcard vendors and souvenir stalls crowd the piazzas, and milling throngs of international visitors cram the streets and museums. Yet among the trappings of modern tourism, the bronze-workers and leather artisans, although dying breeds, can still be found in their workshops.

Evidence of the city's artistic heritage is abundant

Florence's detractors describe the city as overcrowded and overpriced. There is a modicum of truth in such criticism, but the crowds, and to a certain extent the high prices, can be avoided by visiting in low season. You will never escape the overwhelming impact of so much superlative art and architecture, even if you have only a few days to see it. Be selective, pick out a few highlights and absorb them at your leisure. If you try to cover everything you will end up exhausted and remembering little.

TRIALS AND TRIBULATIONS

The medieval Florentines were considered pragmatic, hardworking, inventive and sharp-witted. These qualities are evident in today's inhabitants, along with an innate sense of dignity, elegance and a savage pride in their city and its patrimony.

NOTES

Some of the greatest names in European culture – Dante, Boccaccio, Giotto, Donatello, Botticelli, Michelangelo, Leonardo, Cellini and Machiavelli – lived and worked in Florence. Events and exhibitions continue to celebrate the city's enviable heritage, marking the 500th anniversary of da Vinci's death in 2019 and the 700th anniversary of Dante's in 2021.

The Florentines' resilience has been illustrated throughout history, but never more clearly than during the disastrous flood of November 1966. Swollen by heavy rains, the Arno burst its banks one night, carrying away everything in its wake. In certain parts of the city the water reached depths of 7m (23ft) – small plaques around town indicate the height of the flood. Thick mud, mixed with damaging oil from ruptured tanks, swirled into shops, museums and homes. Hundreds of paintings, frescoes and sculptures, and more than a million priceless antique books were severely damaged, many beyond repair. Before the floodwaters had receded, the people of Florence joined in the Herculean task of rescuing what they could. In the aftermath, they helped to clear debris and repair the urban fabric. Most of the affected works of art are now back on display in Florence's museums and galleries.

The people's resolve was tested once again in May 1993, when a Mafia car bomb tore apart the west wing of the Uffizi Gallery, killing the custodian and her family of four. Irreparable damage to

WHEN TO GO

Florence can be off-puttingly busy in the high season. Midsummer temperatures aren't pleasant, and the number of tourists can make the major attractions a trying experience – although June is more agreeable in terms of both heat and crowds. At this time of year, you will need to reserve your accommodation well in advance. The busiest month is August, when the majority of locals take their holidays, and many restaurants and bars are closed.

Winter is often quite rainy in Florence, and it can be rather cold, but the absence of crowds makes it a good option for the big sights. Pack a raincoat, particularly in the wettest months of October to March. You can snag some great low-season accommodation and flight deals in winter, which can make the winter chill worthwhile.

The shoulder months of spring and autumn are typically less crowded and cheaper than peak summer, but May and September have become increasingly popular months to visit Florence. For the optimal blend of weather, crowds and prices, arrive shortly before Easter or in October.

the collection was limited thanks to protective plexiglass shields. Two hundred works were damaged, 37 of them seriously, and remarkably only two beyond repair. The Uffizi's staff laboured around the clock to put the building back in order while work on the Herculean 'Nuovi Uffizi' (New Uffizi) project, launched in 1989, was resumed apace. Having faced further setbacks, it's now several decades along but at last appears to be approaching completion, rendering the beloved gallery more accessible and greatly expanded in size, allowing for many works that were previously archived to see the light of day.

It is this sense of being custodians of the legacy of the Renaissance, and heirs to an unmatched tradition of excellence, that gives the Florentines an almost Medici-like pride in their city. This feeling of continuity with the past is what makes Florence such a uniquely evocative place. Its unparalleled masterworks are not viewed simply as isolated museum pieces, but in the context of the city that produced them. They are a living record of an extraordinary period of creativity and innovation.

For this reason alone, Florence deserves all the superlatives that are shamelessly showered upon it. What's more, if the heat, crowds and queues become too much, you can always escape to a hilltop across the river, and savour the same view that Michelangelo must have savoured, five centuries ago.

Rental bikes in Florence

SUSTAINABLE TRAVEL

With more than 5 million tourist arrivals in 2023, locals can't be blamed for feeling that Florence has fallen victim to its own beauty. In pushing back on overtourism, however, Florentines have made some strides. Development continues on the Bicipolitana bike path system (with 90+ kilometres of paths now complete). More noticeably, the ZTL (Limited Traffic Zone) continues to keep rental cars out of the city's historic core.

As a visitor, you can help by seeking out only licensed, local tours. Look out for leather workshops, cooking classes and handmade souvenirs. Visit local markets like the colourful Mercato Centrale, the Mercato Nuovo, or Sant'Ambrogio. Select local guesthouses, agriturismos or hotels with European Ecolabel (https://commission.europa.eu) or Green Key (www.greenkey.global) certifications.

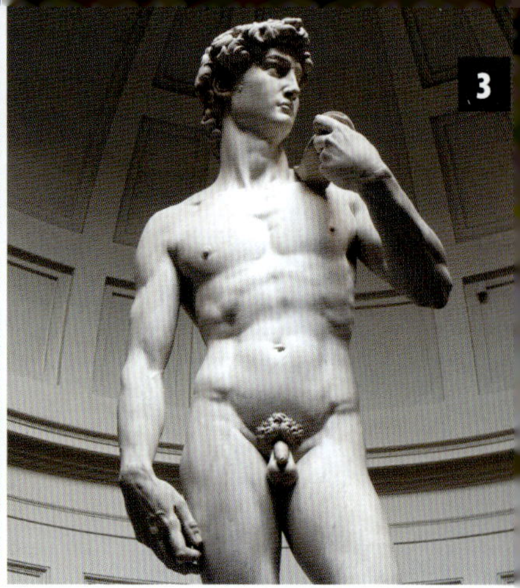

10 Things not to miss

1

2

3

4

5

6

1 THE DUOMO

Brunelleschi's magnificent dome towers above the city; equally impressive is Giotto's graceful campanile. See page 35.

2 PALAZZO PITTI AND GIARDINO DI BOBOLI

A sumptuous palace and delightful pleasure-garden that once belonged to the Medicis. See pages 78 and 80.

3 THE ACCADEMIA

The gallery's star exhibit is Michelangelo's David, perhaps the most famous piece of sculpture in the Western world. See page 69.

4 SANTA CROCE

This glorious church is full of artistic treasures. See page 55.

5 PONTE VECCHIO

The beautiful medieval bridge still retains the small shops of its artisans. See page 77.

6 THE UFFIZI

Home to the world's greatest collection of Italian Renaissance paintings. See page 46.

7 SANTA MARIA NOVELLA

The cavernous church was designed by Dominican architects in the mid-13th century. See page 73.

8 CAPPELLA BRANCACCI

The site of Masaccio's sublime frescoes. See page 82.

9 SAN LORENZO

The first Renaissance church and home to the glorious Medici Chapels. See page 63.

10 SAN MARCO

The frescoed dormitory of the monastery is the location of some of Fra Angelico's finest works. See page 67.

A perfect day in Florence

9.00AM

Breakfast. Start your day with a *cappuccino* and *cornetto* at Caffè Scudieri (see page 117) on the Piazza di San Giovanni (19r). This smart, long-established café/*pasticceria* is right in the heart of Florence, in the pedestrianised Piazza.

10.00AM

The Duomo. Amble around the Piazza, admiring the Baptistery, Campanile (bell tower) and the iconic Duomo (cathedral) with its ancient, underground crypt. Those with stamina can tackle the 463 stairs spiralling to the top of the cathedral's dome to admire Brunelleschi's engineering genius and the fabulous views.

11.30AM

Via de'Tornabuoni. Take the Via Roma south of the Baptistery for Piazza della Repubblica, home to some of the city's most elegant cafés. Cross the square for Via Strozzi and at the end turn left onto Via de'Tornabuoni for the lavish flagship stores of Armani, Gucci and Prada, to name just a few.

1.00PM

Mercato Nuovo. At Piazza Santa Trinità, turn left onto Via Porta, passing halfway along the Palazzo Davanzati. At the end on the right is the Mercato Nuovo; built for the sale of silk and gold, the market is now devoted to leather and souvenirs. Rub the snout of the bronze boar to guarantee your return to Florence and brave a tripe sandwich from the market's southwest corner.

1.30PM

Piazza art. Since medieval times this expansive piazza has been a hub of city life. Overlooking the piazza is the towering Palazzo Vecchio, former ancestral home of the Medici. Admire the array of open-air sculpture, check out the Gucci Garden, or sit at one of the people-watching cafés. For a juicy *bistecca a la fiorentina* and a glass of Chianti, try Frescobaldi (see page 116) next door or Gustavino (see page 116) around the corner.

3.00PM

Ponte Vecchio. Head south for the river, passing the famous Uffizi Gallery, repository of the world's finest collection of Renaissance art. At the River Arno turn right for Ponte Vecchio, Florence's oldest bridge and an iconic symbol of the city. Goldsmiths and jewellers have been selling their wares here since 1593.

3.30PM

Boboli. From the bridge follow the flow to the Palazzo Pitti. The vast palace is home to five museums and could occupy a whole day or more. For now, just explore the lovely Giardino di Boboli, the formal gardens dotted with loggias, cool fountains, grottos and myriad statues.

8.00PM

Dinner time. Make for Piazza Santo Spirito, just northwest of Palazzo Pitti. Relax with an *aperitivo* on the piazza and then choose a spot for dinner.

Florence on a budget

9.30AM

Piazza del Duomo. Arrive early at the city's most celebrated square to admire the Baptistery's bronze "Gates of Paradise" without the thick crowds. Glimpse the Duomo's marvellous facade, Giotto's Bell Tower and Brunelleschi's magnificent dome. Grab an early spot in the line for the church (opens 10.15am) but note that you'll need a ticket to descend to the crypt or scale the cathedral's heights.

11AM

Piazza della Signoria. Heading south, you'll pass through the old Roman forum – today's Piazza della Repubblica – to reach the city's second square: the Piazza della Signoria. An open-air museum, its displays include a marble replica of Michelangelo's *David*, standing outside of the venerable Palazzo Vecchio, whose tower dominates the square. Circle the palace's beautifully frescoed courtyard, adorned with carved pillars, panels and lunettes.

11.30AM

Open-air markets. A block to the east is the Mercato del Porcellino, named for the famous bronze boar, a copy from a Roman marble displayed in the nearby Uffizi. Take part in tourist tradition by tossing a coin in the adjoining fountain and stroking the nose of "the piglet", then follow the Via Por Santa Maria to cross the shop-lined Ponte Vecchio.

12PM

The Oltrarno. Continue south along the old Roman road (now called the Via de' Guicciardini). Barely a minute along, slip into the Church of Santa Felicità just before it closes, spotting inside a pair of noteworthy pieces by the Florentine Mannerist Pontormo. Carry on to the Piazza de' Pitti to glimpse the forbidding exterior of the Medici family's long-time home.

12.30PM

Piazza Santa Spirito. You'll have to pay to glimpse the Church of Santo Spirito's treasured crucifix by Michelangelo (in the sacristy), but not to enter the church. Order a drink to accompany snacks right here in the Oltrarno's prettiest piazza.

4PM

Spectacular churches. Cross the Ponte Santa Trinità headed north, arriving at the square of the same name, adorned with a Roman pillar. Don't miss the dazzling frescoes by Ghirlandaio in the piazza's Church of Santa Trinità. More of the artist's work can be spotted in the Church of Ognissanti, farther up the Arno's bank.

5PM

Sunset vistas. Catch a #12 bus from Piazza d'Ognissanti to be whisked to the hilltop San Miniato al Monte. Stroll to the Piazzale Michelangelo and sit by the terrace's edge to see Florence's most celebrated sunset view.

Renaissance legends

8.30AM

Museo di San Marco. One of the greatest monastic centres during Florence's Golden Age: San Marco was built under the orders of Cosimo (*Il Vecchio*). Its museum houses works by Fra Angelico and Ghirlandaio along with a room considered to have belonged to the friar Savonarola. His firebrand sermons stirred even the dying Lorenzo whose family was soon thereafter expelled from Florence amid an anti-Renaissance fervour.

9.30AM

World-renowned art. After Savonarola's execution, Michelangelo returned to Florence, where he completed *David*, high among the city's most treasured works. Glimpse the original in the Galleria dell'Accademia, reorganized from an academy founded by Cosimo I de' Medici in 1563.

11.30AM

Medici grandeur. Carry on south past the Palazzo Medici Riccardi, the illustrious family's early home, to enter the clearest reflection of the family's power: the Medici Chapels, adjoining the San Lorenzo Basilica. Don't miss either the Old or the New Sacristies, designed by Brunelleschi and Michelangelo, respectively, both masterworks in their own right.

1.15PM

Church of Santa Maria Novella. Escape the noise of Piazza della Stazione by slipping into the cloister of the Church of Santa Maria Novella. Inside, find Masaccio's *Trinity* and admire the exquisite chapels flanking the choir.

2.30PM

Palazzo Vecchio. At the far end of the Piazza della Signoria towers the venerable Palazzo Vecchio, briefly the Medici home. In the upstairs museum, stare up in the Salone dei Cinquecento and spot Michelangelo's *Genius of Victory*, then climb the tower – that imprisoned both Cosimo the Elder and Savonarola for Duomo views.

4.30PM

Basilica di Santa Croce. Passing the artistic trove of the Bargello en route (with work by Donatello and Michelangelo), you'll reach the Piazza di Santa Croce, headed by the church of the same name and filled with breathtaking chapels and the tombs of illustrious Florentines like Galileo Galilei, Machiavelli and Michelangelo. A cenotaph is dedicated to Dante (exiled to and buried in Ravenna).

6PM

Duomo ascent. To gear up for the day's final flourish, down an espresso or rest in a Piazza del Duomo café. Then head to the cathedral's north entrance (reservation required) for the rewarding climb to Brunelleschi's dome. On the way, enjoy views of Vasari's *Last Judgement*, and a close-up encounter with the dome's architectural genius on the narrow, curving ascent to the top.

History

No one quite knows how the Roman town of Florentia came by its name. According to some, it was named after Florinus, a Roman general who in 63 BC encamped on the city's future site to besiege the nearby hill town of Fiesole, ruled by the Etruscans, Italy's pre-Roman lords. Others maintain that the name refers to the abundance of flowers in the region, or perhaps even to the 'flourishing' of the successful riverside town.

Whatever the origin of its name, Roman Florence had developed into a thriving military and commercial settlement by around 59 BC. If you take a walk along the aptly named Via Romana on the south bank of the Arno and cross the Ponte Vecchio towards the city centre, you'll be following in the steps of the Roman legions, travellers and merchants of 2,000 years ago. Though invisible today, all the trappings of civilised Roman life were once located here, including a forum, baths, temples and a theatre. You can see more of this era in neighbouring Fiesole, which has a number of Etruscan and Roman ruins dating to the 1st century BC.

Countess Matilda of Tuscany's tomb

FROM THE CAROLINGIANS TO THE REPUBLIC

A few centuries later, invasions from the north and the

San Miniato's facade dates from the 11th century

fall of the Western Roman Empire (AD 476) plunged Europe into a turbulent period of history. This was briefly relieved by the sway of the Frankish king, Charlemagne, and his vast European empire of the 8th and 9th centuries. However, by the 10th century even greater chaos had set in.

Somehow the Carolingian province of Tuscany survived. In the late 11th century, Florence made rapid commercial and political progress under a remarkable ruler, Matilda, the Grand Countess of Tuscany. The great guilds *(arti maggiori)* came into being in this period. These influential bodies might be seen as the precursors of today's trade unions, set up to protect the interests of the apothecaries and the wool, silk and spice merchants, among others. By 1138, Florence had developed into a self-governing republic and a power to be reckoned with.

At that time, Florence presented an appearance very different from that of today's city. The wealthy merchant families fortified their homes with square stone towers, often more than 70m (230ft) high, to serve as impregnable refuges during the recurring feuds that split the community. By the end of the 12th century, the city's skyline bristled with over 150 towers. Only a few have survived, but a better idea of the town's early appearance can be grasped in the Tuscan hill town of San Gimignano (see page 93).

GUELPHS AND GHIBELLINES

Eventually the interests of an aristocratic elite and a rising merchant class were bound to clash. When they did, Florence's development declined into a series of savage factional struggles. The nobility opposed the broader-based forms of government that the merchants promoted and the situation was aggravated by fierce inter-family feuds and continual raids on Florentine trade by 'robber barons'.

To make matters worse, powerful foreign interests became involved. The pro-Pope Guelph and pro-Emperor Ghibelline parties (see page 23), which first developed in the 13th century, had their origins in other Italian cities where the ambitions of the Papacy and the Holy Roman Empire (founded in AD 962)

Artisans at work, depicted on the church of Orsanmichele

were dangerously divergent. Other Tuscan cities soon followed suit with their own Guelph-Ghibelline factions, and Tuscany remained in a state of turmoil for more than two centuries. Pisa, Lucca, Pistoia, Siena, Arezzo and Florence became in turn enemies or allies, depending on which party held power in which town.

NOTES

The names 'Guelph' (supporters of the Pope) and 'Ghibelline' (supporters of the Holy Roman Emperor) are said to come from the German Welf (dukes of Bavaria) and Waiblingen (the home of the Hohenstaufens) respectively.

EVOLUTION OF FLORENTINE SOCIETY

In spite of these setbacks, Florentine commerce and banking continued to develop, and its woollen-cloth trade prospered. The first gold *fiorino* was minted in the mid-13th century. With the city's patron St Giovanni on one side and the symbolic Florentine lily on the other, it was rapidly adopted throughout Europe as the standard unit of currency.

The city's social evolution during this time was remarkable. Organised 'factories' or workshops were opened. Hospitals, schools and charitable societies were founded. The university, one of Europe's oldest, turned out lawyers, teachers and doctors. Streets were paved, laws were passed regulating noise and nuisance, and the Brotherhood of the Misericordia, a forerunner of the Red Cross, was established (see page 40). Although life was hard and Florence was never a democracy in the modern sense of the word, the city gave its citizens a unique feeling of belonging that overcame class or party differences.

In spite of their internal divisions, the Guelphs gradually edged the Ghibellines out of power. By the late 13th century, the bankers, merchants and city guilds had a firm grasp on the helm of the

Florentine republic and felt secure enough to turn their attention to the building of a fitting seat of government. Already involved with the construction of a sumptuous cathedral, a mighty palace of the people – the Palazzo del Popolo – was begun in 1298. This was later renamed the Palazzo della Signoria and is now known as the Palazzo Vecchio. One of the most handsome surviving structures from this period, it still serves as the city hall, after having followed a brief stint as a Medici residence during the Renaissance.

FLORENCE'S GOLDEN AGE

Florentine bankers now held the purse strings of Europe, with agents in every major city. One group, headed by the Bardi and Peruzzi families, lent Edward III of England 1,365,000 gold florins to finance his campaigns against the French. Then in 1343 the double-dealing Edward suddenly declared himself bankrupt, and toppled the entire banking system.

As always, the resilient Florentines recovered, and the merchant interests set out with ruthless zeal to regain their lost prestige. Despite ceaseless social unrest, violent riots, disastrous floods, and the Black Death of 1347–8, which claimed over half the city's population (and one-third of Italy's), by the early 1400s Florence found itself stronger and richer than ever. The foundation had been laid for its brightest moment to come.

In addition to commercial success, the city's cultural life was flourishing, moving towards the early years of what was to become known as the Renaissance. Interest was reviving in long-neglected Greek and Latin literature. While Florentine historians started recording their city's progress for posterity, merchant guilds and the nouveaux riches found time between business deals and party vendettas to indulge in artistic patronage.

Despite factional divisions, the Florentines were able to plan ambitious public works and awe-inspiring private palazzos. The Duomo, Giotto's Campanile, the great monastic churches of Santa

Croce and Santa Maria Novella, the Bargello and the Palazzo Vecchio were all begun or completed during the tumultuous 14th century.

The power of the important business families, the *signori*, was slowly proving to be greater than that of the guilds. The ambitious Medici, a family of wealthy wool merchants and bankers, came to dominate every facet of Florentine life for 60 golden years (1434–94) and, to a diminishing degree, the decades thereafter. The Medici were shrewd politicians and enthusiastic and discerning patrons of the arts. As patrons they led the city and its people to unparalleled heights of civilisation, at a time when most of Europe was struggling to free itself from the coarse, tangled mesh of medieval feudalism.

Fresco by Filippino Lippi in the Strozzi Chapel of the Santa Maria Novella

THE RENAISSANCE

The term 'Renaissance' *(Rinascimento)* was coined by 16th-century Florentine artist and historian Giorgio Vasari (1511–74), whose book *Lives of the Most Excellent Painters, Sculptors and Architects* tells almost everything we know about the great Italian artists from the 13th century up to his own time. 'Renaissance' means 'rebirth', which is exactly how Vasari saw the events of the 15th century: The world appeared to be waking from a long sleep and taking up life where antiquity had left off. The Church had dominated the cultural life of Europe throughout the Middle Ages. Literature, architecture, painting, sculpture and music were all aimed at the glorification of God, rather than the celebration of earthly life and beauty. The Greek and Roman concept of 'art for art's sake' had been forgotten until it was revived in 15th-century Florence; a comparison of Cimabue's *Virgin Enthroned* (*c*.1290) with *La Primavera* by Botticelli (1477–8) illustrates the difference between the art of the Middle Ages and the Renaissance.

Statue of Lorenzo de' Medici

The idea had firmly taken hold that life must be lived to its fullest and that the pursuit of earthly knowledge, beauty and pleasure were what counted most in the brief time allotted to man. The arts and sciences of the Renaissance were directed towards those ends.

THE MEDICI

Although few of the early Medici ever held office in city government, three of them were in fact the true rulers of Florence. They were: Cosimo, *Il Vecchio* ('the Elder', 1389–1464), a munificent patron of the arts and letters and founder of the Medici dynasty, who earned himself the title *paterpatriae* ('father of his country'); his son, Piero, *Il Gottoso* ('the Gouty', 1416–69); and his grandson Lorenzo, *Il Magnifico* ('the Magnificent', 1449–92). Ably pulling strings via supporters elected to the republican government (the *Signoria*), all three were expert politicians who knew how to win the hearts and minds of the Florentine masses.

> **NOTES**
>
> Poet, naturalist, art collector, dabbler in philosophy and architecture, Lorenzo was perhaps the most outstanding member of the Medici dynasty. He was an example of what is still referred to as a 'Renaissance man'.

Lorenzo's diplomatic skill kept Italy temporarily free of wars and invasions, and his love of the arts had a direct effect on cultural life as we know it today. On Lorenzo's death in 1492, his son Piero, lo Sfortunato ('the Unfortunate'), took his place. Loutish and devoid of taste, Piero lasted just two years. When Charles VIII of France invaded Italy, Piero accepted humiliating terms of settlement. The Florentine people were so enraged that they drove him from the city and set up a republic. It was at this time that Niccolò Machiavelli held office in Florence, gaining first-hand experience in the arts of intrigue and diplomacy.

BONFIRE OF THE VANITIES

The spiritual force behind the new republic was a fanatical Dominican friar from Ferrara, Girolamo Savonarola (1452–98). Prior of the Monastery of San Marco, he preached regularly in the Duomo during Lorenzo's last years. Though at first largely ignored,

FLORENTINE EXPLORERS

Amerigo Vespucci (1454–1512) went down in history as the man who gave his name to America. Banker, businessman and navigator, he crossed the Atlantic in the wake of Christopher Columbus (who was from Genoa), and explored the coast of South America, discovering the estuaries of the Orinoco and Rio de la Plata. His main achievement was to ascertain that Columbus had, in fact, discovered a 'New World', and not Asia, as Columbus himself had maintained.

by 1490, thousands had heard him inveigh against the excesses of the Medici courts, prophesying apocalyptic punishments for the city if its people did not embrace a more godly way of life.

In 1494, he decreed the destruction of the 'vanities' of art, and Florentines flocked to the Piazza della Signoria with armfuls of illuminated books, hand-loomed textiles and precious paintings, which they hurled upon a huge bonfire in the middle of the square. Even Botticelli joined in, flinging some of his own paintings into the flames. But Savonarola had powerful enemies (Pope Borgia, for one) who soon brought about his downfall. He was arrested, sentenced to death for heresy, and hanged and burned where his 'bonfire of the vanities' had taken place four years earlier.

In 1512, Piero's brothers, Giovanni and Giuliano, returned to Florence, putting an end to the republic. Expelled in 1527, the persistent Medici were back three years later, after an eight-month siege, with the help of the Holy Roman Emperor Charles V.

During the subsequent rule of Grand Duke Cosimo I de' Medici (1537–1574), an attempt was made to revive the spirit of the Medici's earlier golden age. Some of Florence's most prominent monuments date from this period, including the Santa Trinità Bridge, the Boboli Garden (Cosimo's back garden when residing in the Palazzo Pitti), the Neptune Fountain in the Piazza della Signoria, and Cellini's magnificent bronze *Perseus*.

THE 18TH AND 19TH CENTURIES

Under the rule of the grand dukes of Tuscany (Medici until 1737, then Hapsburgs up to 1859), Florence sank into a torpor that lasted for more than three centuries. Anna Maria Ludovica, last of the Medici line, who died in 1749, made a grand final gesture worthy of her Renaissance forebears. With foresight she bequeathed the entire Medici art collection to the city 'to attract foreigners', on condition that none of it ever be sold or removed from Florence. This became the basis of the staggering collection of the Uffizi Gallery, formerly the offices of the Medici.

Her wish was granted, for the foreigners came, at first in a small but steady trickle of privileged young gentlemen on the Grand Tour of Europe. However, in the early 19th century a new

Bartolomeo Manfredi's reconstructed 'Card players' from the 17th Century

NOTES

Visitors' opinions about the city have varied widely. Shelley called Florence a 'paradise of exiles', Walter Savage Landor 'the filthiest capital in Europe' and Aldous Huxley 'a second-rate provincial town with… repulsive Gothic architecture'.

breed of traveller appeared, the 'Italianate Englishman', led by the poets Byron and Shelley. Later in the century the Brownings, John Ruskin (although his major work was on Venice), and the Ruskin-inspired Pre-Raphaelites followed. Rapturous Britons, who were smitten by the mythologised and romantic image of Italy, toured or settled in droves, bringing in their wake French, German and Russian tourists, all referred to as 'the English' by the Florentines.

After the dramatic events of the Risorgimento, when the occupying Austrians were expelled, Florence had a brief moment of glory as the capital of the newly unified kingdom of Italy (1865–71). With the later transfer of the capital to Rome, the story of Florence merged into Italian history.

EARLY 20TH CENTURY

Despite the excitement at the time of unification, the early years of independence were turbulent. Political crisis followed crisis, and governments became vulnerable to attack from reactionary forces. During World War I, Italy fought against Germany and Austria, but afterwards the feeling that it had been insufficiently rewarded for its sacrifices was exploited by the fascist Benito Mussolini, who seized power in 1922.

WORLD WAR II TO THE PRESENT DAY

With the Rome–Berlin Axis of 1937, Mussolini linked the fate of Italy to Hitler's Germany, dragging his country to defeat in World War II. The fascist government fell in 1943, with some of the most heroic battles of the Italian resistance fought in and around Florence. The retreating Germans blew up all the bridges over the Arno except for the Ponte Vecchio, while the city's art treasures, and landmark architecture survived unscathed. Mussolini and his mistress were executed in 1945, their bodies displayed in Milan.

Since 1945, Florence has faced a raft of further setbacks and challenges. On November 4, 1966 the Arno broke its banks, causing immense damage to many of the city's artworks and killing 35 people. In 1993, a Mafia bomb exploded by the Uffizi, killing five people and damaging around 200 precious works of art. In more recent years, tourism's steady rise – with 5–6 million annual tourist arrivals – has irked many residents, increasingly displaced by skyrocketing rents that are now among the highest in all of Italy.

Germans display Botticelli's masterpiece, Camilla and the Centaur

Sara Funaro, Florence's current mayor

Since 2009, Florence has had a succession of progressive young mayors from the Democratic Party (PD). Matteo Renzi (2009–2014) reinvigorated the city's political and cultural scene and invested in various eco-friendly initiatives. Almost as soon as he was elected, he announced that the Piazza del Duomo would become a pedestrian only zone. Following Renzi's election as Prime Minister of Italy in 2014, Dario Nardella (2014–2024) took up the reins, overseeing the continued expansion and reconstruction of the Uffizi and the reopening of numerous city landmarks. Like his predecessor, he has prioritized green infrastructure, introducing bike-sharing and electric buses while greatly expanding the tramway network.

In June 2024, the continuation of centre-left dominance was secured for another five years when Sara Funaro became Florence's very first female mayor with more than 60 percent of the vote. She defeated the right-leaning, long-time director of the Uffizi Galleries, Eike Schmidt, whose campaign had stressed law and order. Both campaigns, however, had centred overtourism as among the city's principal challenges, offering plans to ease the strains that have accompanied rising tides of tourists. As reflected in the electoral result, a majority are hopeful that Funaro can lead the way forward now.

CHRONOLOGY

8th century BC The first settlements on the site of Florence.

c.59 BC The foundation of the Roman city of Florentia.

3rd century AD St Minias brings Christianity to Florence.

570 The Lombards take control of Tuscany.

774 Charlemagne defeats the Lombards and takes over Tuscany.

1115 Florence becomes a self-governing commune.

1215 Beginning of the civil strife between the Guelphs and Ghibellines.

1296–9 Work begins on the Duomo and Palazzo Vecchio.

1302 Dante expelled in a mass purge of the Ghibellines.

1347–8 The Black Death kills over half of the city's population.

1400 onwards The beginning of the Renaissance and the rise of Florence as the pre-eminent cultural centre in Europe.

1434–64 Cosimo de' Medici rules Florence.

1469–92 The rule of Lorenzo 'the Magnificent'.

1494–8 Under Savonarola, Florence is a republic under the rule of Christ.

1512 The Medici regain control of the city.

1537–74 The rule of Cosimo I; Florence goes into slow decline.

1610 Galileo made court mathematician to Cosimo II.

1737 The death of Gian Gastone, last Medici ruler of Florence.

1860 Tuscany becomes part of emerging United Kingdom of Italy.

1865–71 Florence is capital of the new kingdom.

1944 The retreating Germans destroy three bridges of the Arno.

1993 A Mafia bomb kills five people and damages the Uffizi.

2002 The euro replaces the Italian lira as the main unit of currency.

2014 Matteo Renzi becomes the Prime Minister of Italy.

2019 Tramvia's Line 2 is inaugurated.

2023 Welcoming 2.4 million visitors, the Uffizi surpasses its pre-pandemic record.

2024 Sara Funaro succeeds Dario Nardella as mayor of Florence.

2026 Projected completion of the decades-long Nuovi Uffizi project.

The Duomo (Santa Maria dei Fiori)

Places

Although Florence's suburbs spread far along the Arno Valley, the old part of the city is compact and easy to negotiate on foot, with most of the sights of interest to visitors. On the northern bank of the River Arno is the *centro storico* (historic centre), laid out around three large squares. Along the western edge of the *centro storico* are three of the city's most important churches, San Lorenzo, San Marco and Santa Maria Novella. Across the river is the district of Oltrarno. Settled later than the north bank, this was once an area of workshops and artisans and still retains a more laid-back air than the heavily touristed streets around the Duomo and Piazza della Signoria.

PIAZZA DEL DUOMO

HIGHLIGHTS

» The Duomo, see page 35
» The Baptistery, see page 39
» Loggia del Bigallo, see page 40
» Museo dell'Opera del Duomo, see page 41

The superb **Piazza del Duomo** is situated to the north of the grid of narrow streets that make up Florence's *centro storico*. At its centre, the magnificent cathedral is the symbolic heart of the city and remains its tallest building.

THE DUOMO

The huge multicoloured facade of the **Duomo** ❶ (https://duomo.firenze.it; closed to visitors Sun; free) rises majestically alongside the pointed roof of the Baptistery.

Officially known as Santa Maria dei Fiori (Saint Mary of the Flowers), the Duomo was designed by the great architect Arnolfo di Cambio (1245–1302), who was also responsible for the Palazzo

WHERE TO SHOOT BEST PICTURES

For good cause, **Piazzale Michelangelo** is easily the most famous sunset spot in town. Come early to claim your spot on the terrace, or climb onwards to San Miniato al Monte, another fabulous vantage point.

Further Florentine panoramas await in the elevated grounds of the **Giardino Bardini** (and particularly, when open, Villa Bardini's third-floor terrace) as well as in the hilltop village of Fiesole and atop Palazzo Vecchio's Torre d'Arnolfo.

From **Ponte Santa Trinita** you can catch the Ponte Vecchio (and the Ponte alla Carraia) reflected in the Arno.

Photographers will certainly find the climb to the top of **Torre Grossa in San Gimignano** worthwhile, offering birds-eye views of the Tuscan hills and the town's medieval towers.

Whether shooting the cathedral in focus or using its inlaid marble facade as a dreamy backdrop, you'll find plenty of eye-popping scenery at **Piazza del Duomo**. To fit Brunelleschi's dome in frame, venture into the side streets (Via dei Servi and Via dello Studio are best).

Vecchio (see page 42). This new cathedral was intended to surpass all of the great buildings of antiquity in both size and splendour.

Work commenced around 1296 on the site of the far smaller 5th-century cathedral of Santa Reparata, but was not completed until the second half of the 15th century. The cathedral's wonderfully elaborate neo-Gothic facade was added as late as the 19th century. Like the majority of Tuscan churches of the time, the Duomo presents a unique local version of Gothic architecture that is not easily compared to other northern European ecclesiastical buildings of the same period.

The mighty **cupola** was the contribution of Filippo Brunelleschi (1377–1446), the first true 'Renaissance' architect, who was inspired by the dome on Rome's Pantheon, rebuilt for Emperor Hadrian in about AD 125.

When the ambitious Florentines decided that their showpiece cathedral must have a great dome, they held a public competition in 1418. Brunelleschi submitted the winning design (encouraged by the organisers to make it *il più bello che si può* – 'as beautiful as possible') and, just as important, architecturally sound. His original wooden model can be seen in the Museo dell'Opera del Duomo (see page 41). In Florence, where beauty and art were never the preserve of the rich alone, these competitions used to cause immense, popular excitement.

Brunelleschi's magnificent dome, the first giant cupola since antiquity, was completed in 1436. It was visible for miles, dwarfing the red-tiled rooftops around it, and confirming the feeling of the day that nothing was beyond the science and ingenuity of man.

The cathedral is Florence's tallest building at 107m (351ft)

By contrast with the polychrome exterior, the cathedral's **interior** is strikingly vast and stark. Although most of the original statuary was long ago moved to the Museo dell'Opera del Duomo, there are still some important works of art to be seen, such as the magnificent 16th-century fresco on the inside of the cupola. The depiction of *The Last Judgement* was begun by Giorgio Vasari and finished by his student Federico Zuccari.

Lorenzo Ghiberti's bronze shrine below the high altar was made to house the remains of St Zenobius, one of Florence's first bishops. The versatile Ghiberti also designed the three stained-glass rose windows on the entrance wall.

Left of the entrance are some unusual *trompe l'œil* frescoes of two 15th-century *condottieri* (mercenary captains) who fought for Florence. The right-hand one, painted by the great master of perspective Paolo Uccello, commemorates an Englishman, John Hawkwood. He was the only foreigner ever buried in the Duomo, although his remains were later repatriated. Uccello is also responsible for the 1443 **ora italica** clock next to Ghiberti's windows.

On the right, just inside the cathedral's entrance, are the steps down to the **crypt** (https://duomo.firenze.it; combined ticket), which contains Brunelleschi's simple tomb.

NOTES

While access to Florence's magnificent cathedral is free, some of the additional attractions inside and around the piazza require tickets, of which various combinations are on offer at (https://duomo.firenze.it), each valid for three days. The most comprehensive of these is the Brunelleschi Pass (€30), including access to the dome, bell tower, baptistery, crypt and the Opera del Duomo Museum. The cheaper Giotto Pass (€20) includes all but the dome and the Ghiberti Pass (€15) excludes both the dome and the bell tower.

The Campanile

Part of Ghiberti's gilded 'Gates of Paradise'

The Duomo's free-standing **Campanile di Giotto** ❷ (https://duomo.firenze.it; combined ticket) is one of Florence's most graceful landmarks. The bell-tower was begun in 1334 by Giotto, and completed in 1359 by his successors Andrea Pisano and Andrea Talenti. Faced in green, white and pink marble to match the Duomo, the lowest storey bears hexagonal reliefs illustrating *Genesis* and various arts and industries by Pisano and Luca della Robbia. The niches in the second storey contain statues of the Prophets and Sibyls, some by Donatello. It is worth making the 414-step climb to the top for a bird's-eye view of the cathedral and a city that was never permitted to build higher than the cathedral's dome.

THE BAPTISTERY

Opposite the Duomo lies **Il Battistero** ❸ (https://duomo.firenze.it; combined ticket). Acclaimed as Florence's oldest building, this precious gem of octagonal Romanesque architecture, served for a time as the city's cathedral. It was built in the early part of the 12th century on what is believed to be the site of a Roman temple. With the exception of its doors, the exterior appearance remains as it was in the time of Dante. Brilliant 13th-century mosaics inside the cupola include scenes from the *Creation*, *Life of St John* and an 8m (26ft) figure of

Christ in the *Last Judgement*. With restoration works ongoing, most of the ceiling mosaics are obscured by scaffolding at present. The current six-year project is slated for completion in 2028.

The Baptistery's principal claim to fame is its three sets of **gilded bronze doors** (originals in the Museo dell'Opera del Duomo). Those on the south side are the oldest. Dating from the 14th century, they are the work of Andrea Pisano. A competition to design another set of doors was held in 1401, financed by one of the merchant guilds. Brunelleschi was among those who submitted an entry, but Lorenzo Ghiberti's submission was declared the winner. Their original entries are now in the Bargello. The first doors Ghiberti produced can be seen on the north side of the Baptistery. The artist later went on to make the magnificent east doors, facing the Duomo and therefore the most important, which were described by an admiring Michelangelo as being fit to be the 'Gates of Paradise'. The name has stuck ever since.

LOGGIA DEL BIGALLO

On the corner of Via dei Calzaiuoli, south of the Baptistery, is the graceful 14th-century **Loggia del Bigallo** (closed for restoration). The loggia (covered gallery) was once part of the headquarters of the **Brotherhood of the Misericordia**, a society for the care of orphans and one of Florence's oldest and most respected social institutions. Founded by St Peter Martyr in 1244, the society was especially needed during frequent bouts of pestilence and plague. Across the street from the loggia lie the brotherhood's current headquarters and a small museum (https://museo.misericordia.firenze.it; charge) housing

NOTES

You can climb up the spiralling 463 steps to the lantern at its top and enjoy breathtaking panoramic views over the city. Entry to the steps is via the Porta della Mandoria (https://duomo.firenze.it; combined ticket; time slot selection required) on the northern side of the Duomo.

some fine works of art. Today's unpaid volunteers, easily recognised in their black hooded capes, provide free assistance to the poor and needy, and also run an ambulance service.

The imposing Palazzo Vecchio

MUSEO DELL'OPERA DEL DUOMO

At the east end of the piazza, the **Museo dell'Opera del Duomo** ❹ (https://duomo.firenze.it; closed first Tue of the month; combined ticket), holds many of the Duomo's most precious treasures and original sculptures in its 28 rooms, which are spread over three floors. After 27 years of restoration, the original bronze panels of Ghiberti's Gates of Paradise, designed for the Baptistery, were finally put together in 2015. The gates are on display at the Salone del Paradiso; the grandest hall of the revamped museum. The sumptuous 14th–15th-century silver-faced altar is also from the Baptistery. Other treasures include rich gold and silver reliquaries, one of which supposedly houses the index finger of St John, Florence's patron saint. Brunelleschi's original wooden model of the Duomo's cupola is also here, as is Donatello's harrowing wooden effigy of Mary Magdalene and the *Zuccone* that once graced the Campanile. The two beautiful, sculptured choir lofts (*cantorie*) are by Donatello and Luca della Robbia respectively. The museum also houses Michelangelo's unfinished *Pietà*, which may have been intended for his own tomb.

PIAZZA DELLA SIGNORIA

HIGHLIGHTS

» Palazzo Vecchio, see page 42
» Loggia dei Lanzi, see page 45
» The Gucci Garden, see page 46
» The Uffizi, see page 46
» The Museo Galileo, see page 51

The second major square of the *centro storico* is **Piazza della Signoria** ❺. If the Piazza del Duomo is the religious heart of Florence, this piazza is its political and social counterpart. The city rulers have gathered here since the 13th century, and the present-day offices of the city council are still housed in the austere Palazzo Vecchio.

PALAZZO VECCHIO

Dominating the square is the fortress-like **Palazzo Vecchio** ❻ (https://ticketsmuseums.comune.fi.it; courtyard: free; museum and tower: charge, separate tickets), also known as the Palazzo della Signoria after the highest tier of the city's 15th-century government, the *Signoria*, which convened here. Designed in 1299 by Arnolfo di Cambio, who also designed the Duomo, it was intended to house the city's government. After serving briefly as a Medici residence, it acquired the name Palazzo Vecchio (Old Palace) in 1550 when the Medici moved their headquarters over the river to the new Palazzo Pitti (see page 78). The palazzo's off-centre 94m (308ft) tower, added in 1310, helps to soften the building's squareness and complements its off-centre position on the piazza.

The palazzo's interior comes as a surprise after the medieval austerity of the exterior. It was completely remodelled when Cosimo I de' Medici moved in, in 1540. The **courtyard,** designed by Michelozzi Michelozzo in 1453, is delightful. Vasari, who also designed the fountain at the centre, added the ornate stucco and frescoes in 1565.

The palazzo's inner courtyard, designed by Michelozzo in 1453

Verrocchio's bronze fountainhead depicting a putto with a dolphin was brought here from Lorenzo de' Medici's villa at Careggi. What you see here is a copy; the original is displayed upstairs.

Most of the palazzo's highlights are contained in the upstairs **museum**, beginning with the first floor's massive **Salone dei Cinquecento**. Built to house the parliament of the short-lived Florentine republic declared in 1494, Cosimo I later turned it into a grand throne room. He had it decorated with giant Vasari frescoes of Florentine victories and Michelangelo's statue *The Genius of Victory*, representing Cosimo's triumph over enemy Siena in 1554–5. Three centuries later, the first parliament of a united Italy met here. It is still used today for special government functions.

A small door to the right of the main entrance leads into the **Studiolo di Francesco I** (only accessible on a guided tour), a little gem of a study designed by Vasari. It is covered from floor to barrel-vaulted ceiling with painted allegorical panels (representing *Fire, Water, Earth* and *Air*), and two Bronzino portraits of Cosimo I and his consort gazing down haughtily.

Across the hall, another door leads into the **Quartiere di Leone X**, the apartments of the first Medici pope. The rooms are sumptuously decorated with frescoes celebrating the achievements of the Medici family. Stairs lead up to the equally sumptuous **Quartiere degli Elementi**, with painted allegories on the theme of the elements. The Terraza di Saturno at the back provides a fine view across the river.

A gallery above the Salone dei Cinquecento leads to the **Quartiere di Eleonora** (the apartments of Cosimo I's Spanish wife), a riot of gilt, painted ceilings and rich furnishings.

The splendid 15th-century **Sala dei Gigli** (Hall of the Lilies), all blue and gold, is lavishly decorated with Florentine heraldry, a gilt-panelled ceiling, bright Ghirlandaio frescoes, and superb doors inlaid with figures of Dante and Petrarch. Here stands Donatello's original bronze of *Judith and Holofernes*. A copy is in the piazza outside.

Next door is the splendid **Sala Mappamondo,** a cupboard-lined room

Giambologna's Abduction of the Sabine Women

whose wooden panels were painted with maps by two learned Dominican friars (1563–87).

Before descending, you can climb the soaring **Torre d'Arnolfo** (94m; 308ft), a Florentine symbol, reached via 223 steps and affording some of the finest views in all of Florence. Along the climb you'll pass the cell where the firebrand cleric Savonarola awaited his execution in the square below.

LOGGIA DEI LANZI

On the south side of the Piazza della Signoria is the Loggia della Signoria, more commonly known as the **Loggia dei Lanzi**, built in the late 14th century. Originally a covered vantage point for city officials at public ceremonies, it took its later name from Cosimo I's Swiss-German mercenary bodyguards, known as *Landsknechts* (Italianised to *Lanzichenecchi*), who used it as a guardroom during his nine-year residence in the Palazzo Vecchio. Since the late 18th century, the loggia has officially been an open-air sculpture museum, but celebrated works of art have been displayed here since long before then. Cellini's fine bronze *Perseus* was originally placed here, on Cosimo's order in 1554. Giambologna's *Abduction of the Sabine Women* was added in 1583, while his *Hercules and the Centaur* and the Roman statues at the back, donated by the Medici, were added towards the end of the 18th century.

In front of the palazzo a *marzocco* – a heraldic lion bearing the city's arms (the symbol of Florence) – has graced the piazza for almost as long as the palazzo itself. What you see today is a copy; the original is in the Bargello. Michelangelo's *David* was positioned here in 1504 as a republican symbol, but was moved to the Accademia (see page 69) in 1873 and replaced with a copy. The present version is an early 20th-century copy; a bronze version can be found across the river in the Piazzale Michelangelo. The rather grotesque statue of *Hercules and Cacus*, beside *David*, is the work of 16th-century sculptor, Bandinelli.

THE GUCCI GARDEN

The **Gucci Garden** (www.gucci.com; charge) housed in the historic Palazzo della Mercanzia provides light relief from Renaissance sculpture. The Gucci Garden Galleria tells the story of the brand in a number of themed rooms while the Gucci Osteria da Massimo Bottura restaurant and Gucci store complete the scene.

THE UFFIZI

Between the Palazzo Vecchio and the Arno, the **Galleria degli Uffizi** ❼ (Uffizi Gallery; www.uffizi.it; closed Mon; charge) stretches down either side of the narrow Piazzale degli Uffizi. This was Vasari's greatest architectural work. Built in the second half of the 16th century, the building was intended to house the headquarters of various government offices (*uffizi* is Old Italian for 'offices'), the official mint and workshops for Medici craftsmen. It is now the home of one of the world's most famous and important art galleries.

There are usually long queues to get in, and the gallery can be very crowded. To avoid the queues, book a timed entrance ticket in advance online or by phone.

The Uffizi has been undergoing a massive and painfully slow redevelopment since 1989. Rather than close entirely, the work has advanced piecemeal, with sporadic rearrangements and final completion of the Nuovi Uffizi slated for 2026. The ongoing project will double the number of paintings on show and allow twice as many visitors to the gallery. Check the website for current closures.

Exhibited in chronological order, the paintings comprise the cream of Italian and European art from the 13th to 18th centuries. Begun by Cosimo I and added to by his successors, the collection was bequeathed to the people of Florence in perpetuity in 1737 by Anna Maria Ludovica, the last of the Medici dynasty, on condition that it never leave the city.

A visit begins on the second floor, where the first rooms contain those early Tuscan greats, **Cimabue** and **Giotto**. In their altarpieces

'The Birth of Venus' by Sandro Botticelli in the Uffizi Gallery

depicting enthroned Madonnas (painted in the 1290s and early 1300s, respectively), the mosaic-like stiffness of Cimabue's work contrasts vividly with Giotto's innovative depth and more expressive figures. One of the greatest painters of the 14th-century Sienese school was **Simone Martini**. This claim is evidenced by his graceful *Annunciation* (1333; room A5), painted for Siena's cathedral. Of the later Italian Gothic masterpieces, the *Adoration of the Magi* (1423; A7) by Gentile da Fabriano is the most exquisite. Of the early Renaissance works, do not miss the large and exciting depiction of the *Battle of San Romano* (1456; A9) by Uccello, or the paintings by Masaccio.

Among the most loved and reproduced of Renaissance paintings are the haunting *La Primavera* (The Allegory of Springtime; *c.*1480) by **Botticelli** (room A11) and his renowned *Birth of Venus* (commonly referred to as 'Venus on the Half-Shell',

Michelangelo's Doni Tondo

c.1485; A12). Botticelli's life-like but theatrical *Adoration of the Magi (A13)* features portraits of the Medici family – Cosimo Il Vecchio, his son Piero Il Gottoso and grandsons Lorenzo Il Magnifico and Giuliano (standing smugly on the extreme left, a few years before his murder). Botticelli himself, in a yellow cloak and golden curls, gazes out on the far right.

In the same room is a huge 15th-century Flemish triptych by **Hugo Van der Goes**, *The Adoration of the Shepherds* (1478), which was painted for the Medici's Flemish agent, Tommaso Portinari.

A couple doors down is the sumptuous **Tribuna,** an octagonal room symbolising the four elements, commissioned by the Medici from Bernardo Buontalenti. The 17th-century inlaid stone table, specially made for the room, took 16 years to complete. Since its renovations (completed in 2012), visitors can view but no longer access the room.

Among the most recently rearranged (reopened in 2024), the next rooms host the museum's collection of Renaissance treasures from Northern Europe, with works by masters such as Dürer, Cranach, Froment and Memling. Don't miss the *Adoration of the Magi* (1504) by **Dürer** and *Adam and Eve* (1526) by **Cranach.**

Entering the western corridor series, you'll next find a series of rooms devoted to stars of the High Renaissance era, among them

Leonardo da Vinci (Room A35). *The Baptism of Christ* (c.1470–5) was mostly the work of his great teacher, Verrocchio. Although only the background and the angel on the left were the work of the 18-year-old Leonardo, when Verrocchio saw how exquisitely his pupil had rendered the angel, he swore never to touch a paintbrush again. The *Annunciation* (1475) is entirely Leonardo's work, as is the *Adoration of the Magi* (1482). Representing the works of the 15th-century Venetian School is the strange, dream-like *Sacred*

RENAISSANCE ARTISTS

Although the glimmerings of humanism can be seen in the works of Cimabue and Giotto, the Renaissance is said to have truly arrived when Brunelleschi submitted his design for the Baptistery doors in 1401. Although beaten by Ghiberti in the competition, Brunelleschi's relief of Abraham and Isaac is more dynamic and depicts the human drama of the story. Brunelleschi's most lasting legacy to the city is in architecture, especially his Duomo, Spedale degli Innocenti and the Pazzi Chapel, but he is also credited with the invention of measured perspective.

In sculpture, pride of place goes to Brunelleschi's friend Donatello (1386–1466), whose bas-relief on the plinth of his *St George* at Orsanmichele shows early use of perspective, and whose David was the first free-standing male nude since antiquity.

In painting, the Renaissance was ushered in by Masaccio (1401–28), with his solid, modelled human figures, followed by Paolo Uccello (1397–1475), master of perspective, and the melancholic Filippo Lippi (1406–69). In the realm of religious art, the outstanding figures were Andrea Verrocchio (1435–88), Leonardo da Vinci's teacher and a fine sculptor; Domenico Ghirlandaio (1449–94), famous for his frescoes; and the exquisitely lyrical Botticelli (1444–1510). The High Renaissance saw the arrival of three master artists who epitomise the period: Leonardo da Vinci (1452–1519), artist and scientist; Michelangelo (1475–1564), sculptor, architect, painter and poet; and Raphael (1483–1520), a gifted painter.

Allegory (A34), painted about 1490 by Bellini. Its allegorical significance has never been fully explained.

The Uffizi contains just one work by the great **Michelangelo**, a round oil painting showing the Holy Family, known as the *Doni Tondo* (1503–5; A38). Firmly but humanly treated, it is the only known panel painting by an artist better known for frescoes and sculpture. The same room also displays Raphael's *Madonna del Cardellino* (c. 1505).

At the end of the corridor, a terrace with a view of the **Duomo** offers a scenic rest before continuing to the first floor. For the full circuit, take the stairs nearest the terrace, leading to the museum's expansive, diverse collection of **self portraits**, first compiled in the 1600s and now showcasing 255 works.

Alternatively, a shorter route descends via the Buontalenti staircase, skipping ahead to where the second floor left off: around the turn of 16th century. Among the celebrated works here are **Titian**'s voluptuous nude, the *Venus of Urbino* (1538; D23), and the great Medici family portraits by Bronzino (D14–17).

The tour concludes by breaching the Baroque era, with the paintings of **Caravaggio** taking pride of place, among them *Medusa* (1597), *Bacchus* (c. 1598) and the *Sacrifice of Isaac* (c. 1603). There are also great 17th-century works from much farther afield such as **Rembrandt**'s *Portrait of an Old Man* (1665) – reflecting the reach and impact of the artistic flourishing spawned here in Florence several centuries prior.

NOTES

The Corridoio Vasariano is a graceful, covered walkway built by Vasari in 1565, running from the Uffizi and over the Ponte Vecchio to the Medici's new headquarters in the Palazzo Pitti. It allowed Grand Duke Cosimo de' Medici to commute between the two without ever braving the elements or brushing shoulders with the populace. After lengthy renovations, the corridor was reopened to the public in 2024 (www.uffizi.it; reservation required).

THE MUSEO GALILEO

The state-of-the-art **Museo Galileo** ❽ (www.museogalileo.it; charge) is a welcome change after over-indulgence in the arts. Renaissance Florence was an important centre of scientific research, and Cosimo II hired the best mathematicians, astronomers and cartographers from all over Europe and the Middle East. On display are their beautifully engraved astrolabes and armillary spheres, showing the motion of the heavenly bodies. Other treasures include mahogany and brass reconstructions of Galileo's experiments and fascinating 15th- and 16th-century maps and globes that show how rapidly new discoveries were revolutionising our understanding of the world.

David by Donatello, Bargello Museum

THE BARGELLO AND SANTA CROCE

HIGHLIGHTS

- The Bargello, see page 52
- Badia Fiorentina, see page 54
- Piazza Santa Croce, see page 54
- Cappella dei Pazzi, see page 57
- Casa Buonarroti, see page 58

The Horne Museum, see page 58East of Piazza della Signoria is **Piazza San Firenze.** This small square is dominated by the towering Baroque facade of **San Firenze**, the seat of Florence's Law Courts.

THE BARGELLO

On the northern edge of the square is the forbidding, fortress-like Palazzo del Bargello, home of the **Museo Nazionale del Bargello** ❾ (https://bargellomusei.it; closed Tues; charge). This was Florence's original town hall and one of its earliest public buildings, begun around 1250. The Bargello served as the seat of the magistrates (*podestà*) responsible for law and order, and later housed the office of the Captain of Justice (*bargello*), the 16th-century equivalent of today's police commissioner. Today, the Bargello is to sculpture what the Uffizi is to painting, for it houses many Renaissance masterpieces.

The first room beyond the entrance is the **Sala Michelangelo** where marks on the wall record the water level of the 1966 flood at 3m (9ft). Michelangelo was only 21 when he finished his early masterpiece, *The Drunken Bacchus*. He sculpted the marble *Pitti Tondo* of the Virgin and Child eight years later in 1504, while working on his famous *David* (now in the Accademia). You will also find Michelangelo's 'other David', *Apollo*, sculpted 30 years after the original.

A 14th-century stone staircase leads to an arcaded loggia on the first floor, where you'll see Giambologna's series of remarkably lifelike bronze birds surrounding a marble figure representing *Architecture*.

The first-floor exhibits include Italian and Tuscan ceramics, old Murano glass, French Limoges enamels and astonishing, delicate engraved seashells. The 14th-century chapel contains frescoes painted by a pupil of Giotto. The man behind the kneeling figure on the right is said to be Dante.

If you are pressed for time, head straight for the **Salone di Donatello**, which contains works by the sculptor that captures the spirit of early Renaissance Florence. Donatello's movingly human *St George* (1416) dominates the back wall of this impressively high-vaulted room. It was commissioned by the armourers' guild as their contribution to the exterior decorations of Orsanmichele. The sculpture's depth and sense of movement are generally believed to represent the first great sculptural achievement of the Renaissance.

Museo Nazionale del Bargello

Donatello's most important work – his bronze figure of *David* (1440–50) – is credited as the first free-standing nude statue of the Renaissance. In contrast to the 'modern' feeling of *St George*, his *David* has an antique and ambiguous sensuality about it, while the delightful bronze *Amore* (Cupid) is positively Roman in style. More personal and dramatic are the two marble versions of *St John the Baptist*.

Be sure to take a look at Ghiberti and Brunelleschi's original bronze panels (*The Sacrifice of Abraham*), designed for the Baptistery design competition of 1401; they're on the right wall towards the back of the room.

The Sala di Verrocchio on the second floor has Verrocchio's bronze David (*c.*1471), which may have been modelled on the sculptor's 19-year-old pupil, Leonardo da Vinci. Also on the second floor is the model for Giambologna's *Abduction of the Sabine Women* in the Loggia dei Lanzi.

Santa Croce's neo-Gothic facade

BADIA FIORENTINA

Across the street from the Bargello is the church known as the **Badia Fiorentina** (entrance on Via Dante Alighieri; closed Mon morning; donation), with its graceful bell-tower; part Romanesque, part Gothic. Go inside for a moment to admire Filippino Lippi's delightful *Madonna Appearing to St Bernard*, on the left of the church as you enter.

From the southern end of Piazza San Firenze, take the Borgo dei Greci. This crosses **Via de' Bentaccordi**, one of the few curved streets in medieval Florence. It owes its shape to the fact that it once ran round the outside of Florence's Roman amphitheatre. At the far end of Borgo dei Greci you can see the black and white facade of Santa Croce.

PIAZZA SANTA CROCE

The vast expanse of **Piazza Santa Croce** formed one of the social and political hubs of Renaissance Florence, but is mostly a residential neighbourhood today. Lorenzo and Giuliano de' Medici used to stage lavish jousts here, and defiant Florentines turned out in force during the 1530 siege to watch or take part in their traditional football game (re-enacted here every summer). The buildings on the right-hand side of the square, with their cantilevered upper floors, were typical of the late medieval city.

The cavernous Franciscan church of **Santa Croce ⑩** (www.santacroceopera.it; closed to visitors Sun morning; charge) started off in 1210 as a modest chapel, situated in the middle of a working-class district. Arnolfo di Cambio, the architect of the Palazzo Vecchio and the Duomo, drew up the plans for a larger church, which was completed in the 14th century. The interior, beneath its open roof-beams, is grandly Gothic, while the facade is 19th-century neo-Gothic.

The church is the last resting place of some of the most illustrious figures in Italian history, many of them born in Tuscany. Just inside the door on the right is the **tomb of Michelangelo,** designed by his first biographer, the 16th-century artist and architect Giorgio Vasari. The seated figures on the monument represent, from left to right, *Painting*, *Sculpture* and *Architecture*.

The next tomb on the right wall is that of Dante Alighieri. It lies empty, much to the dismay of Florence. A Florentine by birth, Dante was exiled for political reasons. His body lies in Ravenna, where he died; the city has never given in to Florentine pleas for its return (a statue to him stands just outside Santa Croce's main entrance). Farther along is the tomb of Niccolò Machiavelli (1469–1527), civil servant, political theorist, historian and playwright. Gioacchino Rossini

Tomb of Dante Alighieri

DANTE

Dante Alighieri, the father of Italian literature, was born in Florence around 1265. As a consequence of his Guelph allegiances, he was exiled from Florence for the last 19 years of his life and threatened with death by burning if he returned to the city. Though this sentence was repealed in 2008, his body remains in Ravenna and his tomb in Santa Croce lies empty.

Dante's immortal poetic work, *The Divine Comedy*, describes a journey through Hell and Purgatory to arrive at last in Paradise. One of the great landmarks of world literature, it juxtaposes divinely ordained political and social order with the ugly reality of the corrupt society that surrounded the poet in the early 1300s. Dante was the first to write his masterpiece not in the usual scholarly Latin, but in his everyday language. He thus established the Tuscan vernacular as the 'pure Italian' spoken today and used as the language of literature.

(1792–1868), Florentine by adoption and the composer of *The Barber of Seville* and *The William Tell Overture*, is also buried here.

Opposite Michelangelo is the tomb of Galileo Galilei (1564–1642), shown holding the telescope that he invented. A plaque on the front of the Pisan's tomb depicts the four moons of Jupiter that he discovered with the use of the instrument. On the same side of the church, beside the fourth column from the door, lies sculptor Lorenzo Ghiberti, creator of the famous Baptistery.

A tranquil chapel in the left transept houses a coloured wooden Christ on the cross, carved by Donatello. His friend Brunelleschi mockingly dismissed the sculpture as 'a peasant on the cross'; Brunelleschi's answer can be found hanging in the Church of Santa Maria Novella. The honeycomb of family chapels on either side of the high altar contains a wealth of frescoes dating from the 14th to 16th centuries. To the right of the altar, in the **Bardi Chapel**, (closed for restorations at the time of writing) are Giotto's finest and arguably most moving works – scenes from the life of

St Francis, painted around 1320. The adjoining chapel contains Giotto frescoes of the life of St John, commissioned by the Peruzzi, rich bankers who donated most of the money for the church's imposing sacristy. A fragment of tunic supposedly belonging to St Francis is displayed here.

CAPPELLA DEI PAZZI

In the cloister adjoining the church of Santa Croce's right side is the small but exquisite **Cappella dei Pazzi** ⓫ (www.santacroceopera.it; entry included). The once-tarnished reputation of the Pazzi family (resulting from the assassination of Giuliano Medici in the Duomo), was redeemed by their commission of this Renaissance masterpiece, designed by Brunelleschi in 1443. It contains his glazed terracotta decorations of the four Evangelists and the tondos (circular works of art) of the 12 Apostles by Luca della Robbia. The former refectory houses a museum (entry included) containing frescoes and statues that were removed from the church for preservation, but its greatest treasure is Cimabue's massive 13th-century painted crucifix. Restored after near-destruction in the 1966 flood, it hangs from heavy cables that can raise it out of harm's way at the push of a button.

Battle of the Lapiths against Centaurs, 1490–2, by Michelangelo

CASA BUONARROTI

Close to Santa Croce are two more interesting museums. The **Casa Buonarroti** (Via Ghibellina 70; www.casabuonarroti.it; closed Tues; charge), was bought by Michelangelo as an inheritance for his heirs. He lived for a short period of time in one of three small houses eventually combined to create the current residence. It contains letters, drawings and portraits of the great man, as well as a collection of 17th-century paintings illustrating his long, productive life. The exhibits include his famous sculptured relief the *Madonna of the Staircase*, completed before the artist was 16. His astonishing *Battle of the Lapiths and Centaurs* dates from around the same time.

THE HORNE MUSEUM

Situated near the river at Via de' Benci 6, the **Museo Horne** (www.museohorne.it; closed Wed; charge) is a superb little 15th-century palazzo, restored, briefly lived in, and eventually bequeathed to the city of Florence in 1916 by the eccentric Englishman Henry Percy Horne. On display is his priceless collection of Italian Renaissance art, ceramics and furniture. The museum is also the meeting point and ticket office for visits to the last home of the artist, architect and writer, Giorgio Vasari (1511–1574), set just around the corner.

PIAZZA DELLA REPUBBLICA

HIGHLIGHTS

- Via Tornabuoni and Piazza Santa Trinità, see page 60
- Palazzo Davanzati and Mercato Nuovo, see page 61
- Orsanmichele, see page 61

To the west of Piazza della Signoria is the third major square of the *centro storico*, the grand **Piazza della Repubblica** ⓬, built on the site of the old Roman forum. Florence was capital of Italy from 1865–71, after which the capital was transferred to Rome. A

Piazza della Repubblica, once the site of the Roman forum

jumble of medieval buildings was cleared during the 19th century to create the square, as part of the project to create a fitting capital for the newly independent state. The piazza's stylish cafés fill up at lunchtime with office workers from the surrounding banks and businesses, and there is usually live music on summer evenings.

If you leave Piazza della Repubblica by Via degli Strozzi, just before the end of the street on the left you will see the massive walls of the **Palazzo Strozzi** (www.palazzostrozzi.org; charge), begun in 1489 as a private residence. Wrought-iron torch holders and rings for tethering horses are set in the masonry, but the cornice above the street remains unfinished, along with other details, since money for construction ran out after the death of Filippo Strozzi. The palace hosts three blockbuster exhibitions annually and is open year-round with a café/bar and a permanent exhibition on the palace.

VIA TORNABUONI AND PIAZZA SANTA TRINITÀ

Via degli Strozzi leads to the pedestrianised **Via Tornabuoni** ⓭, one of Florence's main shopping streets, lined with the boutiques of the city's fashion houses. At the southern end of the road is the **Piazza Santa Trinità**. On the western side of the piazza is the fine 16th-century facade of the church of **Santa Trinità** ⓮ (free) by Bernardo Buontalenti. The Gothic interior comes as a complete surprise. It was built between the 13th and 15th centuries on the site of an older Romanesque church, the remains of which are still visible. Look for the late 15th-century Sassetti Chapel (second on the right from the chancel), with scenes from the life of St Francis by Ghirlandaio.

Outside the church, in the centre of the piazza, is the **Colonna della Giustizia** (Column of Justice), a granite pillar taken from the Baths of Caracalla in Rome. It was erected by Grand Duke Cosimo I de' Medici to celebrate his victory over a band of exiled Florentines anxious to overthrow him and re-establish a more democratic government.

Loggia del Mercato Nuovo

Many wealthy families lived in the area, building impressive palazzos and sponsoring richly frescoed chapels. The exquisite, early 16th-century **Palazzo Bartolini-Salimbeni** and the 13th-century fortress-like **Palazzo Spini-Feroni** both stand on the piazza. The latter has been unofficially renamed the Palazzo

Ferragamo, after the local family whose expanding empire of fashion and style is now located within the palazzo. The **Museo Salvatore Ferragamo** (https://museo.ferragamo.com; charge) in the basement displays lavish shoes created for the likes of Marilyn Monroe and Greta Garbo by the famous shoe designer, Salvatore Ferragamo.

NOTES

To the south of the Mercato Nuovo is *Il Porcellino* (the piglet), a 17th-century bronze statue of a boar, copied from a Roman marble original now in the Uffizi. Legend has it that if you stroke his nose and toss a coin into the fountain, you will return to the city.

PALAZZO DAVANZATI AND MERCATO NUOVO

East of Piazza Santa Trinità, on Via Porta Rossa, is the **Palazzo Davanzati** ⓯ (https://bargellomusei.it; closed Mon; charge). The palazzo's museum gives a fascinating insight into life in medieval Florence. The dour exterior belies a splendid, colourful interior, especially the living quarters with their gorgeous wall hangings, frescoes and painted ceilings.

The Via Porta Rossa leads on to the **Mercato Nuovo**. A market has existed here since the 11th century; the main attraction today is the profusion of stalls selling bags, belts, small leather goods and assorted souvenirs. The current arcade was built in 1547–51 for the sale of silk and gold. It remains a lively place attracting both locals and tourists alike.

ORSANMICHELE

North of the market, on Via della Calzaiuoli, is the unusual church of **Orsanmichele** ⓰ (https://bargellomusei.it; closed Tues; charge). The original building was an open-sided loggia, like the Mercato Nuovo, and was rebuilt in 1337 by the silk guild for use as a market. It was converted to a church in 1380, and in the early 15th century the two

Inside Orsanmichele church

upper storeys were added and used as an emergency granary. In the rear left-hand corner of the ceiling you can see the ducts through which grain was poured. Mystical and mysterious, the pillared interior is dominated by Orcagna's splendid 14th-century altarpiece, built around an allegedly miracle-working image of the Madonna.

Adopted by the city's wealthy merchant and craft guilds, the church's square, fortress-like exterior was embellished with Gothic-style niches and statues during the late 14th and early 15th centuries. Each guild paid for one of the 14 niches and commissioned a statue of its patron or favourite saint. Those in the church itself are now copies but the originals can be seen in the first floor's museum.

On the north side of the church is a copy of Donatello's *St George*. The original is in the Bargello. Commissioned by the armourers' and sword-makers' guild, this work was one of the first masterpieces of Renaissance sculpture. Particularly revolutionary at the time was the relief-work of St George killing the dragon, carved on a panel beneath the main statue.

Copies of Ghiberti's statues of *St Matthew* and *St Stephen* can be seen on the west side, opposite the impressive 13th-century **Palazzo dell'Arte della Lana**, once the headquarters of the powerful wool merchants' guild.

SAN LORENZO

HIGHLIGHTS

- The Medici Chapels, see page 64
- The Mercato Centrale and Palazzo Riccardi, see page 66

This area to the north of the Duomo was home to the Medici dynasty for centuries and is the final resting place of all of the family's most important figures.

The rough-hewn dark stone structure of **San Lorenzo** ⓱ (charge) looks like a huge Tuscan barn. Financed by the Medici, the prestigious project was built by Brunelleschi between 1425 and 1446, while its facade was to be completed by Michelangelo. He completed the interior but never delivered the planned external marble facings. The artist's model is on display at the Casa Buonarroti museum. For once at least, 19th-century architects did not try to finish the job.

Florence's first entirely Renaissance church and one of Filippo Brunelleschi's earliest architectural triumphs (before he built the Duomo's cupola), the building was begun on the site of a 4th-century basilica. Cosimo Il Vecchio later had his palace built within sight of the church (the Palazzo Medici-Riccardi, with its entrance on Via Cavour). He liked to consider the Church of San Lorenzo as the Medici's parish church.

A door in the left wall of the church leads to the cloister and the stairs up to one of Michelangelo's architectural masterpieces, the **Biblioteca Medicea Laurenziana** (Laurentian Library; also accessible by a door to the left of the front entrance to the church; www.bmlonline.it; closed weekends; charge). A monumental staircase climbs to the **reading room** (phone reservation only; tel: 055-293 7911), graced with a splendid wooden ceiling and earthy terracotta floor. Commissioned by Pope Clement VII in 1524 to house a precious collection of Medici books and manuscripts, it was opened to the public in 1571 and is one of the world's most beautiful libraries.

The sober church of San Lorenzo was the burial site of many of the Medici. Cosimo Il Vecchio himself is in the crypt beneath the dome, while his parents are in the Old Sacristy, along with his two sons, Piero Il Gottoso and Giovanni, in a sumptuous porphyry-and-bronze tomb by Verrocchio. Donatello is buried in the left transept. A giant of early Renaissance art, he decorated the Brunelleschi-designed Old Sacristy.

THE MEDICI CHAPELS

San Lorenzo is best-known and most visited for the sumptuous Medici tombs, found in the **Cappelle Medicee** ⓲ (Medici Chapels; https://bargellomusei.it; closed Tues; charge). The entrance is

A splendid fresco inside San Lorenzo's dome

via Piazza Madonna degli Aldobrandini amid a jumble of stalls from the daily outdoor tourist market. From the crypt, filled with the tombs of minor family members, a staircase leads up to the **Cappella dei Principi**. This early 17th century Baroque extravaganza, added on after the completion of the New Sacristy, was intended to be the family burial vault to surpass all others. The workmanship of multicoloured inlaid marble and semi-precious stones is astounding, even if by today's standards it looks a little over-the-top. Six huge sarcophagi bear the mortal remains of some lesser-known Medici (left to right from the entrance): Cosimo III, Francesco I, Cosimo I, Ferdinando I, Cosimo II and Ferdinando II.

Follow the stream of visitors to the main attraction, the **New Sacristy** (*Sagrestia Nuova*), reached via a corridor beside the stairs. This is an amazing one-man show by Michelangelo, who spent more than 14 years designing the interior and creating seven of the sculptures. Commissioned in 1520 by the future Pope Clement VII (the illegitimate son of Giuliano de' Medici) as a resting place for both his father (killed in the Duomo during the Pazzi conspiracy) and uncle (Lorenzo Il Magnifico), it also accommodated two then recently deceased cousins (Giuliano, Duke of Nemours, and Lorenzo II, Duke of Urbino). In a cramped little space beneath the sacristy, charcoal sketches were unveiled in 1975, attributed to the maestro himself. It's believed that Michelangelo hid in this **secret room** for several weeks in 1530, evading a death sentence (soon rescinded). The room can now be visited in groups of no more than four (reservation required; tel: 055-294 883). Having started in 1521, Michelangelo continued working on the Sacristy until 1534; Vasari finished it in 1556.

The two more illustrious members of the Medici clan are buried to the right of the entrance, beneath Michelangelo's fine *Virgin and Child*, which is flanked by figures of the Medici patron saints, Cosmas and Damian. Ironically it was the two lesser cousins who were immortalised by Michelangelo with two of the most famous funeral monuments of all time.

Detail of the Tomb of Lorenzo de Medici, by Michelangelo

On the right stands an idealised, war-like Giuliano, Duke of Nemours, above two splendid figures symbolising *Night* (female) and *Day* (male), reclining on an elegantly curved sarcophagus. On the right, the unfinished face of *Day* still shows the marks from Michelangelo's chisel, making the figure all the more remarkable.

Night is accompanied by the symbols of darkness – an owl, a mask, the moon, and a sack of opium symbolising sleep. Opposite, a pensive Lorenzo, Duke of Urbino, sits above *Dawn* (female) and *Dusk* (male). The pairing of these figures enhances the overall drama and complexity of this monumental tomb, representing the cycle of life and death.

THE MERCATO CENTRALE AND PALAZZO RICCARDI

Just north of San Lorenzo, the busy, leather-scented street market of Via dell'Ariento and the late 19th-century covered **Mercato Centrale** add a dose of local colour. East of San Lorenzo on Via Cavour is the massive **Palazzo Medici-Riccardi** ⓳ (entrance on Via Cavour; https://www.palazzomediciriccardi.it; closed Wed; charge; entrance to the chapel is limited to 10 visitors every 5 minutes, so be prepared to queue). In 1439, Cosimo Il Vecchio, founder of the Medici dynasty, commissioned Brunelleschi's student Michelozzo to build the first home of the Medici clan, where they would live until 1540 when Cosimo I moved to the Palazzo Vecchio (see page 42) and then to the Palazzo Pitti (see page 78). Today it houses Florence's Prefecture, guarded by *carabinieri* (police).

The palazzo's ground-floor museum is often used for special exhibits, but its real attraction is the renovated Cappella dei Magi on the first floor. The chapel contains Benozzo Gozzoli's famous fresco, the *Procession of the Magi*, painted 1459–63. The work is a lavish pictorial record in rich, warm colours of everybody who was anybody in 15th-century Florence, including the whole Medici clan and a self-portrait of the light-blue-hatted artist.

SAN MARCO

HIGHLIGHTS

- Galleria dell'Accademia, see page 68
- Piazza della Santissima Annunziata, see page 69
- The Foundling Hospital, see page 70
- Museo Archeologico and Tempio Ebraico, see page 71

North of the city centre, facing onto Piazza San Marco, is the Dominican church and monastery of **San Marco**. Adjoining the church (closed Sun morning to visitors; free) is one of Florence's most evocative museums: the **Museo di San Marco** ⓴ (https://museitoscana.cultura.gov.it; closed 1st, 3rd and 5th Sun of the month and Mon following 2nd and 4th Sun of the month; charge). The Florentine-born early-Renaissance painter Fra Angelico (1387–1455) lived here as a monk. Most of his finest paintings and frescoes, including the great *Deposition* altarpiece, can be seen in the Pilgrim's Hospice *(Ospizio dei Pelligrini)*, to the right of the entrance. Follow signs to the small Refectory (*Refettorio*), decorated with a vivid Ghirlandaio mural of *The Last Supper*, a favourite subject for monastery dining halls and one of seven in Florence.

The cloister bell resting placidly in the Sala della Capitolo has had a chequered career. Donated by Cosimo de' Medici, it was known as *La Piagnona* (The Great Moaner). In the 15th century, Girolamo Savonarola was the monastery's fire-and-brimstone preacher, prior and sworn enemy of the Medici. His puritanical supporters tolled the bell to alert the monks when an angry mob came to arrest him in 1498, earning them the nickname *I Piagnoni*. For its act of treason, the bell was condemned to 50 years of exile outside the city, and was whipped through the streets all the way out of town.

Upstairs in the dormitory, you can visit the monks' cells, each one bearing a fresco by Fra Angelico or one of his pupils. His masterpiece, the famous *Annunciation*, is at the top of the stairs; another version can be found in cell No 3. At the end of the row to the right of the stairs are cells 38 and 39, once reserved for Cosimo de' Medici's meditations. At the farthest end of the dormitory are the former quarters of Savonarola.

Piazza San Marco

The architect Michelozzo expanded the 13th-century monastery in 1437. His superb colonnaded library leads off the dormitory and is now used for rotating exhibits.

GALLERIA DELL'ACCADEMIA

At the east end of Piazza San Marco is a 14th-century loggia and the entrance to the Accademia di Belle Arti (Fine

Arts). Founded by Cosimo I in the 16th century, the school was enlarged in 1784 with an exhibition hall and a collection of Florentine paintings. The entrance to the **Galleria dell'Accademia** ㉑ (www.galleriaaccademiafirenze.it; closed Mon; charge) is on Via Ricasoli, south of the loggia.

NOTES

On the eastern side of San Marco is the delightful **Giardino dei Semplici**, also called the **Orto Botanico** (www.msn.unifi.it; closed Mon; charge). Now part of the university, the garden was begun by Duke Cosimo in 1545 and was initially used to grow medicinal herbs, hence its name. Today tropical plants and Tuscan flora have been added to the collection.

The gallery's main attraction is its seven sculptures by Michelangelo, whose standout centrepiece is the 4.5m (15ft) ***David,*** perhaps the most famous sculpture in the Western world. Brought here from the Piazza della Signoria in 1873, it is displayed in a purpose-built domed room. Commissioned in 1501 as a symbol of Florence, upon its completion Michelangelo was just 26 years old. The balanced and harmonious composition and mastery of technique instantly established his *David* as a masterpiece. Cleaned in 2004, the marble has regained its original lustre, adding to its impact.

The other works here are the four *Prisoners*, providing a remarkable illustration of Michelangelo's technique as they emerge from the rough stone. He claimed that all his sculptures already existed within the block of marble, and that he only had to release them. These figures, apparently struggling to break out of the rough marble that holds them captive, offer a wonderful expression of his philosophy.

PIAZZA DELLA SANTISSIMA ANNUNZIATA

From the Piazza San Marco, a walk along Via C. Battisti leads to the **Piazza della Santissima Annunziata** ㉒, Florence's prettiest square and perhaps the finest example of Renaissance architecture and proportion in the city.

Brunelleschi probably designed the piazza, with graceful colonnades on three sides, when he built the square's Spedale degli Innocenti in the early 1440s. On the north side, the church of **Santissima Annunziata** (free) was completed in 1481; its architect, Michelozzo, conformed to the piazza's original design, ensuring lasting harmony. The square's spacious feeling is added to by the two 17th-century fountains by Tacca, and Giambologna's equestrian statue of Grand Duke Ferdinando I.

The church entrance leads to an atrium decorated with frescoes by Andrea del Sarto, among others, from which a door opens into the extravagantly decorated interior. Immediately left of the entrance, the 15th-century shrine of the Annunziata shelters an old painting of the *Annunciation*, displayed only on special feast days and said in legend to be painted by a monk with the help of an angel. Reputed to have miraculous properties, it has been the object of pilgrimages and offerings for centuries.

Michelangelo's masterpiece

THE FOUNDLING HOSPITAL

The **Museo degli Innocenti** ㉓ (www.museodegl innocenti.it; charge), housed in Florence's Foundling Hospital (*Spedale degli*

MICHELANGELO'S DAVID

The promising young Michelangelo had just completed the *Pietà*, now on display in Rome's St Peter's Basilica, when he was commissioned to sculpt his *David* in 1501. Of all his works, this masterpiece is most immediately associated with the Florentine master, who will forever be considered the Renaissance's most influential force. One detractor, the 19th-century Grand Tourist and essayist William Hazlitt, described it as 'an awkward overgrown actor at one of our minor theatres, without his clothes'. Those who come today to stand in quiet awe are more inclined to agree with D.H. Lawrence, who considered it 'the genius of Florence'. A life-size marble copy stands in front of the Palazzo Vecchio in the Piazza della Signoria, while a bronze replica anchors the hilltop Piazzale Michelangelo, where the magical sunset views over Florence are the same as those that influenced Florence's most famous son over 500 years ago.

Innocenti means 'Hospital of the Innocents') on the east side of the square, presents three themed exhibitions devoted to art, architecture and history. Built to Brunelleschi's design in the 1440s, this was the first foundling hospital in Europe. Note the 15th-century glazed terracotta roundels of swaddled babes by Andrea della Robbia on the arched facade. These are the 'della Robbia babies' that so appealed to Lucy Honeychurch, the heroine of E.M. Forster's novel *A Room with a View*. Under the northern end of the colonnade is the small door where abandoned babies were once left.

MUSEO ARCHEOLOGICO AND TEMPIO EBRAICO

The archway to the left/north of the Spedale leads out of the piazza and to the Via della Colonna and the **Museo Archeologico** ㉔ (https://museitoscana.cultura.gov.it; closed Sun except for 1st Sun of the month; charge). Housed in what was once the palace of a grand duke, the museum holds important collections of ancient Egyptian, Greek and Etruscan art, especially the collection

One of Andrea della Robbia's babies on the Spedale degli Innocenti

of bronzes that includes the famous *Chimera* (5th century BC). The superbly reconstructed Etruscan tombs in the gardens were damaged in the 1966 flood but have since been restored.

Beyond the Archaeological Museum, just off Via della Colonna on Via Luigi Carlo Farini, is the **Jewish Synagogue and Museum** (*Tempio Ebraico*; www.jewishtuscany.it; closed Sat; charge). Florence's huge Jewish synagogue is easily recognised by its green, copper-covered dome. It was built in the Hispano-Moroccan style between 1874 and 1882 on the site of the ghetto, founded by Cosimo I in 1551. Ghetto, meaning 'slag' or 'waste', was first coined in Venice in the 1500s, referring to foundry on the Venetian island where Venice's Jews were confined. Segregation was the rule at the time in a hostile Europe where Jews, as non-Christians, were viewed as alien, and only some Italian city-states granted refuge.

SANTA MARIA NOVELLA

HIGHLIGHTS

- Santa Maria Novella, see page 73
- Museo Marino Marini and Cappella Rucellai, see page 75
- Ognissanti, see page 75

The first view of Florence for travellers emerging from the railway station is the slender campanile of Santa Maria Novella rising prominently across the square. This is only the back view of one of Florence's greatest monastic churches; to fully appreciate the intricate beauty of its multicoloured marble facade you must take a short walk around into **Piazza Santa Maria Novella.**

SANTA MARIA NOVELLA

The cavernous church of **Santa Maria Novella** ㉕ (www.smn.it; last entry to the church complex 1hr before closing; charge) was designed by Dominican architects in the mid-13th century. A small Dominican community still resides within its walls. In 1470 the architect Leon Battista Alberti completed the upper part of the bold, inlaid marble front in Renaissance style.

Walk beneath the soaring vaults of the 100m (328ft) tall nave to the cluster of

The Holy Trinity, by Masaccio

NOTES

Before leaving Piazza Santa Maria Novella, note the stone obelisks supported by Giambologna's bronze turtles. They marked the boundaries of horse races and chicken races common from approximately 1550–1850.

richly frescoed family chapels surrounding the altar. The chancel is decorated with a dazzling fresco cycle by Ghirlandaio depicting *Scenes from the Lives of the Virgin and St John*, which was paid for by the wealthy Tornabuoni family. Ghirlandaio, Florence's leading 'social' painter of the late 15th century, peopled his biblical frescoes with members of the Tornabuoni clan – one of whom was the mother of Lorenzo Il Magnifico – all dressed in the latest everyday fashions.

To the right of the altar are the **Filippo Strozzi Chapel**, colourfully frescoed by Filippino Lippi, son of the painter Fra Filippo, and the **Bardi Chapel**, with 14th-century frescoes. **The Gondi Chapel** to the left of the altar contains a Brunelleschi crucifix, a response to Donatello's 'peasant' crucifix in Santa Croce and his only work in wood. On the extreme left is the **Strozzi Chapel**, with 14th-century frescoes of *The Last Judgement, Heaven* and *Hell*. Its benefactors, of course, are depicted in Heaven.

The church's most striking work is Masaccio's *Trinity* (*c.*1427) on the wall of the left aisle. Famous for the first such handling of early perspective and a convincing illusion of depth, the fresco depicts the crucifixion in a purely Renaissance architectural setting, dramatically breaking from the established canons of religious art.

Museum and Cloisters

The renovation of Santa Maria Novella's **museum** (combined ticket with the church), arranged around the cloisters, added a new entrance from the station square, among other improvements. The great 14th-century cloister with its three giant cypresses is known as the **Chiostro Verde** (Green Cloister) after the greenish tint of the frescoes of the *Universal Deluge* by Paolo Uccello. Nearby the **Cappellone degli Spagnoli** (Spanish Chapel) is an impressive, vaulted chapter-house named in honour of Cosimo I's Spanish wife, Eleonora of Toledo. Gigantic 14th-century frescoes cover its four walls. The artist incorporated a picture of the Duomo complete with its cupola – 60 years before it was actually completed. Treasures from the monastery are housed in the large, vaulted Chapter House.

MUSEO MARINO MARINI AND CAPPELLA RUCELLAI

South of Piazza Santa Maria Novella, the Via dei Fossi – lined with antiques shops – leads down to the riverside **Piazza Goldoni**. A little way down Via dei Fossi on the left, Via della Spada leads to the **Museo Marino Marini** (www.museomarino marini.it; charge). Set in the deconsecrated San Pancrazio church, the museum has an excellent collection of the 20th-century sculptor's work. Accessed from the museum is the Rucellai Chapel. Attributed to Alberti, this is a tiny scale model of the Church of the Holy Sepulchre in Jerusalem, with decorative and symbolic marble inlay.

Inside Santa Maria Novella church

OGNISSANTI

From Piazza Goldoni, Borgo Ognissanti leads towards

NOTES

A 15-minute walk west along the river from Ognissanti will bring you to Le Cascine, a pleasant park that runs along the embankment west of the city for 3km (2 miles). *Cascina* means 'dairy farm', and that is what it was until it was acquired by Duke Alessandro de' Medici then laid out as a park by his successor, Cosimo I.

the church of **Ognissanti** (All Saints; https://chiesaognissanti.it; closed Tues; free). The church dates from around 1250, contrary to the impression given by its fine 17th-century facade and the della Robbia glazed-terracotta relief over the doorway. Its builders, the *Umiliati* (Humble Ones), were a monastic community who, ironically, ran a remarkably lucrative wool business and were among the first to put Florence on the road to financial prosperity.

The church contains Botticelli's *St Augustine*, and in the Refectory, Ghirlandaio's other famous *Last Supper (Cenacolo)* (closed afternoons; timetable varies month to month; free). The wealthy Vespucci family commissioned both pieces. The family's most famous member was the navigator and cartographer, Amerigo, who lent his name to the New World. Several family members are buried here, as is Botticelli himself.

THE OLTRARNO

HIGHLIGHTS

- Ponte Vecchio, see page 77
- Palazzo Pitti, see page 78
- Santo Spirito, see page 82
- Santa Maria del Carmine, see page 82
- Piazzale Michelangelo and San Miniato al Monte, see page 83

The district on the south bank of the river, called the **Oltrarno** (beyond the Arno), contains some of Florence's most characterful neighbourhoods.

PONTE VECCHIO

Florence's oldest bridge, the **Ponte Vecchio** ㉖ was the only one spared destruction in World War II. Its banks were bombed, as evidenced by the 1950s buildings at either end, but the bridge remained intact. The present bridge dates to 1345 and is lined with jewellers' and goldsmiths' workshops that overhang the river. From the terrace in its middle, you can look west towards the softly curved arches of the elegant **Ponte Santa Trinità**. One of the many bridges blown up by the retreating Germans in August 1944, Trinità

The Ponte Vecchio

was carefully reconstructed, exactly as Ammannati had designed it in the 16th century.

Via de' Guicciardini passes the church of **Santa Felicità** (free) on the way towards Piazza de' Pitti. Inside are two works by the Mannerist artist Pontormo (1494–1557), an *Annunciation* and a *Deposition.*

PALAZZO PITTI

On Piazza de' Pitti is the huge **Palazzo Pitti** ㉗ (www.uffizi.it; closed Mon; a single, cumulative ticket grants entry to all museums on the palace grounds). The Florentine merchant Luca Pitti, who wanted to impress his rivals, the Medici, built this palace as a symbol of wealth and power. Begun in 1457, it was continuously enlarged until the 19th century. Pitti died (together with his savings) in 1472, but the Medici were sufficiently impressed by his palace to buy it in 1549, enlarging it substantially. It then served as the official residence of the Medici (beginning with Cosimo I and his wife Eleonora of Toledo) and the successive ruling families of Florence until 1919, when it was bequeathed to the country. An exploration of the palace's museums

THE MEDICI VILLAS AND GARDENS

UNESCO-listed since 2013, a constellation of rural escapes dot the countryside around Florence, built by and for the Medici family, eminent patrons of the Renaissance. The Giardini di Boboli is the largest of these and the nearest to the city in the Oltrarno. Of roughly a dozen other country estates and gardens situated farther afield, several are both worthwhile and within easy reach. About 5km north of the centre, the Villa La Petraia features an elaborate courtyard, lavish apartments and a medieval tower, while the nearby Villa di Castello boasts innovative gardens and the striking, artificial Grotto of Animals. Perched in the Tuscan hills about 15km west of town is the Villa di Poggio a Caiano, home to stunning 16th-century frescoes by Pontormo. Find visiting information for each villa at https://villegiardinimedicei.it.

and grounds can stretch to several hours.

Palatine Gallery and Royal Apartments

The sumptuous **Galleria Palatina** and the **Appartamenti Reali** (Palatine Gallery and Royal Apartments; first floor) are the main attractions of the Palazzo Pitti complex. The latter consists of 14 lavishly decorated rooms. Its name is misleading as the inhabiting families were not in fact monarchs. The former preserves the magnificent art collection of the Medici and Lorraine grand dukes, just as the owners hung them. It is a grand jigsaw puzzle jumbled by theme and personal preference rather than historical sequence. Priceless paintings decorate dazzling rooms, hung four-high amid gilded, stuccoed and frescoed decoration. It is the largest and most important collection of paintings in Florence after the Uffizi. There are superb works by masters such as Titian, Rubens, Raphael, Botticelli, Velázquez and Murillo, exhibited in grandiose halls adorned with ceiling paintings of classical themes, such as the Hall of the Iliad and the Hall of Venus.

Galleria Palatina at the Palazzo Pitti

The Modern Art, Costume and Medici Treasury Museums

The best of 19th- and 20th-century Italian art can be seen in the interesting **Galleria d'Arte Moderna** (Gallery of Modern Art; www.

uffizi.it; charge; single ticket for all Palazzo Pitti collections), on the floor above the Palatina. Here you can discover the exciting works of Tuscany's own Impressionist movement, the *Macchiaioli* (or 'spot-painters') of the 1860s. In 1999, 100 new paintings were added to the already fascinating collection. On the same floor is the **Museo della Moda e del Costume** (Museum of Costume and Fashion; www.uffizi.it; charge; single ticket for all Palazzo Pitti collections), which showcases haute couture from the 18th century to the present day.

On the ground floor, sixteen sumptuous rooms comprise the **Tesoro dei Granduchi** (Treasury of the Grand Dukes), which displays some of the Medici's most cherished jewellery, gold, silver, cameos, crystal, ivory, furniture and porcelain, including the priceless collection of 16 exquisite antique vases that belonged to Lorenzo Il Magnifico. The room in which they are displayed is the biggest surprise of all, with 17th-century frescoes that create a dizzying optical illusion of height and depth. Also on the ground floor in the former summer apartments are the **Museo delle Icone Russe**, a superlative collection of 17th-century Russian icons, and the Hapsburg Lorraine family's beautifully frescoed **Palatine chapel**.

Piazza Santo Spirito

The Garden and the Porcelain Museum

Once you've seen the galleries, take a relaxing stroll in the delightful **Giardino**

di Boboli ㉘ (charge separate from other Palazzo Pitti attractions, though combination ticket available), an Italian pleasure-garden of arbours and cypress-lined avenues. Along with a dozen other outlying villas and gardens originally laid out by the Medici family, the site was inscribed in 2013 as a UNESCO World Heritage Site (see page 78). The entrance to the gardens at the back of the palace courtyard, leads to the amphitheatre, which has fine views.

NOTES

It is said that Florentine artists young and old made pilgrimages to the Brancacci Chapel to marvel at and learn from Masaccio's achievement (stories recount visits by Michelangelo and Leonardo, who sat and sketched).

Up the hill behind it are the Vasca del Nettuno (Neptune Fountain) and the Palazzina detta 'del Cavaliere', housing the **Museo delle Porcellane** (Porcelain Museum; temporarily closed). Off to the right, at the end of a long cypress avenue, is the Piazzale dell'Isolotto, an idyllic island of greenery, fountains and sculpture set in an ornamental pond.

Returning downhill, head right just below the amphitheatre to see the **Grotta di Buontalenti** (temporarily closed for restoration). A fake grotto full of sculptures, it also contains the much-photographed statue of Cosimo I's court jester, depicted as a pot-bellied dwarf riding on the back of a turtle.

Giardino Bardini

A footpath from the Giardino di Boboli leads to the **Giardino di Bardini** (same ticket as Giardino di Boboli). Less crowded than the Boboli Gardens, the manicured gardens rise up in terraces towards Piazzale Michelangelo, featuring statues, grottoes, fountains and fine views over Florence. The gardens can also be accessed from Via dei Bardi, near the **Museo Stefano Bardini** (see page 83).

SANTO SPIRITO

Turn left out of the Palazzo Pitti and walk up to the nearby Piazza San Felice and then right along Via Mazzetta to see the attractive, tree-lined **Piazza Santo Spirito**. Arrive before 2pm to explore the piazza's morning fruit and vegetable market, or to watch the trade from one of the pavement cafés. On the second Sunday of each month an antiques market takes over.

The modest pale-golden facade rising gently above the back of the piazza is the beautiful church of **Santo Spirito** ㉙ (www.basilicasantospirito.it; closed Wed; free), an Augustinian foundation dating all the way back to the 13th century. The present church was designed by the great Brunelleschi and built in the second half of the 15th century. The bare, unfinished exterior conceals a masterpiece of Renaissance architectural harmony. The interior's walls are lined with 39 elegant side altars, while slender stone columns with Corinthian capitals, arches and vaulted aisles interplay to create an impression of tremendous space. A small charge grants access to the sacristy, which houses a crucifix carved by Michelangelo.

SANTA MARIA DEL CARMINE

Further west is the unpretentious church of **Santa Maria del Carmine**. The church houses some seminal Renaissance frescoes commissioned by the wealthy merchant Felice Brancacci. From 1425–27, a young Masaccio and his teacher Masolino worked on the decorations of the **Cappella Brancacci** ㉚ (https://ticketsmuseums.comune.fi.it; closed Tues, Sun morning; maximum of 30 visitors are allowed in at one time, for 30 minutes, advance booking required) at the end of the right transept. Beautifully restored in 2023, Masaccio's chapel is now approached via a separate entrance through the adjoining cloister to the right of the church's entrance. Masolino's own work is striking enough, but Masaccio's *The Tribute Money* and *The Expulsion of Adam and Eve from the Garden of Eden* raised the art of painting to an unprecedented level. His feeling for light and space, his dramatic stage-set figures, and the solidity of their forms were considered little short of an inspired miracle. Their creation heralded the arrival of the Renaissance.

A devastating fire in 1771 somehow left the Brancacci frescoes intact, but elsewhere in the church you will see the late Baroque architecture and styling used to recreate the church. Opposite the Brancacci Chapel is the Corsini Chapel, a rare jewel of Florentine Baroque style.

The interior of Brancacci Chapel

PIAZZALE MICHELANGELO AND SAN MINIATO AL MONTE

Back at the Ponte Vecchio, the Via dei Bardi leads east to the Piazza Santa Maria Soprarno. A little farther along is the lovely **Museo Stefano Bardini** ㉛ (https://cultura.comune.fi.it; charge). Antiques dealer Stefano Bardini created his palazzo over a church and monastery, incorporating fragments of the ancient buildings. He bequeathed the palace and his eclectic art collection to the city in 1923. Among the highlights are Bernardo Daddi's monumental crucifix, a terracotta altarpiece by Andrea della Robbia, a *Madonna* that is attributed to Donatello and Pollaiuolo's *St Michael*.

Continuing east along Via di San Niccolò and a right turn up Via San Miniato will bring you to Porta San Miniato, one of the few surviving gateways from the 14th-century city wall. On the other side of the wall, follow Via dei Bastoni until you reach a set of stone steps on the right that leads straight uphill, passing through leafy gardens and interrupted occasionally by a switchback road. At the top of the series of steps is the **Piazzale Michelangelo** ㉜. If you cannot manage or face the climb, buses 12 and 13 run up the hill from Ponte San Niccolo and Piazza d'Ognissanti. The square was laid out in the 19th century and is dotted with reproductions of Michelangelo's sculptures, not to mention scores of tour buses and souvenir stalls. The views are absolutely marvellous; it is from here that all those classic postcard pictures of the rooftops of Florence are taken.

The church of **San Miniato al Monte** ㉝ (https://sanminiatoalmonte.it; free), arguably the most beautiful in Florence and beloved by Florentines, enjoys a magnificent hilltop location above Piazzale Michelangelo. St Minias, an early Christian martyred during the 3rd century AD, is said to have carried his own severed head up to this hilltop and set it down on the spot where the church was later built. Rebuilt in the early 11th century, it is a remarkable example of Florentine-style Romanesque architecture. The superb green-and-white marble facade, visible from Florence below, contains a 13th-century mosaic representing Christ flanked by St Minias and the Virgin Mary. The cool, mystical interior has all the

Roman theatre at Fiesole

splendour of a Byzantine basilica, with its wealth of richly inlaid marble and mosaic decorations. Note the painted wooden ceiling, and the nave's 13th-century oriental-carpet-like marble pavement.

Beside the church, the **Cimetero Monumentale delle Porte Sante** dates back to 1864, when burials in the historic centre of Florence were banned. Look for the tomb of Tuscan-born Carlo Collodi (born Lorenzini), the author of *Pinocchio*.

EXCURSIONS

HIGHLIGHTS

- Fiesole, see page 85
- Pisa, see page 87
- Siena, see page 90
- Santa Maria della Scala, see page 93
- San Gimignano, see page 93

Within easy reach of Florence are some of Tuscany's most impressive attractions, all accessible on a day trip. On the hills above the city is the village of Fiesole, and in the neighbouring Chianti district the spectacular towers of San Gimignano. A little farther afield are the modern cities of Pisa and Siena, both powerful city-states in their day, the latter a great rival to Florence.

Like Florence, Pisa and Siena celebrated their success through patronage of the arts, evolving their own visual styles and amassing troves of artistic and architectural treasures.

FIESOLE

A winding road climbs for some 8km (5 miles), weaving through the outlying neighbourhoods north of Florence to reach the charming little hilltop town of **Fiesole** 34 (take the No. 7 bus from Stazione Nazionale). An ancient Etruscan stronghold and later a Roman settlement, it provides a peaceful escape from the

Cathedral of Pisa in Piazza dei Miracoli

city's sweltering summer heat and bustling crowds. Additionally, it boasts wonderful views over Florence and the Arno Valley, making it a must-visit destination for those seeking stunning vistas.

Piazza Mino

The bus drops you in the central **Piazza Mino,** which has a market on Saturdays and a couple of pleasant cafés. Opposite the bus stop is Fiesole's cathedral. Founded in 1028 and completed during the 13th and 14th centuries, **San Romolo** (free) was totally restored in the 19th century, leaving it with a rather drab exterior. Its campanile, visible for miles around, dates back to 1213. A Byzantine atmosphere pervades the interior, which contains the Capella Salutati, with two works by Mino da Fiesole – a tabernacle showing the *Virgin with Saints*, and the tomb of Bishop Salutati.

East of the cathedral is the **Teatro Romano** and the **Area Archeologica** Ⓐ (www.museidifiesole.it; closed Tues; charge: combination ticket includes Bandini Museum). The well-preserved theatre dates from around 100 BC and seats some 2,500 spectators, with stunning views. Half original and half restored, it is the site of a popular arts festival held in July and August. Below the theatre are the remains of the Roman baths and a temple. A small but interesting archeological museum is housed in a replica of the temple inside the entrance. Just opposite the site is the **Museo Bandini** (www.museidifiesole.it; included in combined ticket) with a collection of paintings by the Italian Primitives.

From the square, follow the signs for the extremely steep but picturesque **Via di San Francesco**, which climbs to the church of **San Francesco** Ⓑ (www.parrocchiasanfrancescofirenze.it; free) and its tiny monastery. The views of Florence from the terrace below the church are gorgeous. The monastery, its quirky antiquities museum and peaceful little cloisters, are enchanting. A wooded park offers a choice of footpaths back down the hill.

Between Fiesole and Florence

From the southwest corner of the Piazza Mino, the steep **Via Vecchia Fiesolana**, the original road to the town, zigzags down the hillside towards Florence. Over the centuries various villas have been built here to take advantage of the breathtaking views, including the **Villa Medici**, built here in 1458–61 by Michelozzo for Cosimo de' Medici.

You rejoin the main road at the 15th-century Dominican church and monastery of **San Domenico** (free). Fra Angelico took his vows here; his fine fresco of *The Crucifixion* adorns the Chapterhouse.

Just before the church, a right turn leads to the **Badia Fiesolana** (www.eui.eu; free), a former monastic complex which housed Fiesole's cathedral until 1028. Rebuilt by Cosimo Il Vecchio in the 15th century, it is a gem of Renaissance architecture.

From San Domenico it is possible to catch the No. 7 bus or enjoy the pleasant 4km (2.5-mile) walk downhill through the Mugnone Valley and back to central Florence.

PISA

Roughly 80km (50 miles) west of Florence lies **Pisa** ㉟, the birthplace of Galileo, and home of the fabled Leaning Tower. The city was a flourishing commercial centre and port during the Middle

Ages, until the silting-up of the Arno estuary left it stranded 11km (7 miles) inland from the coast. The most conspicuous legacy of Pisa's wealthy and powerful past, and what everybody comes to admire, is the architectural wonders of the **Piazza dei Miracoli** (Square of Miracles), also known as the Piazza del Duomo. The miracles in question are the Duomo itself, the Battistero, the Camposanto and, of course, the cathedral's circular campanile, the Leaning Tower.

The centrepiece of the Field of Miracles is the white marble **Duomo** (Cathedral; www.opapisa.it; free). This was the most important and influential Romanesque building in Tuscany, and the first to use the much-copied horizontal 'banding' of grey-and-white marble stripes. It was begun *c.*1063 and completed by the 13th century; the bronze doors facing the tower date from 1180. The striped decoration is repeated in the vast interior, which also boasts an ornate wooden ceiling. The cathedral's masterpiece, however, is the magnificent carved pulpit by Giovanni Pisano (1302–10), son of the famous sculptor Nicola Pisano. Opposite the pulpit is the 16th-century **Galileo Lamp,** whose workings inspired his theory of pendulum movement. The apse's dazzling mosaics depicting **Christ Pantocrator** were finished in 1302 by Cimabue.

The **Battistero** (Baptistery; www.opapisa.it; combined ticket for visiting several Piazza dei Miracoli monuments) was started in 1152 but not completed until the 14th century. The sparsely decorated interior, famous for its excellent acoustics, contains a superb hexagonal pulpit carved in 1260 by Nicola Pisano, father of Andrea and Giovanni.

However, it is the world-famous, 57m (187ft) campanile of the cathedral, the **Torre Pendente** (Leaning Tower; www.opapisa.it; combined ticket for Piazza dei Miracoli monuments), which really captures the eye, just as beautiful and delicate as carved ivory, and now leaning by 4.1m (13.5ft). Begun after the Duomo and Baptistery in 1173, the campanile began to lean when only three of the eight storeys had been completed, since the shifting ground beneath the Campo is waterlogged sand – hardly ideal foundation material (the Duomo and Baptistery are also marginally off kilter). Various architects attempted to correct the lean as construction work continued, resulting in a slight bend by the time of the tower's completion in 1372. A remarkable engineering project in the 1990s and early 2000s saved the tower from collapse, reducing the lean by about 50cm (1.6ft) and purportedly stabilizing the structure for the next 200 years.

On the north side of the piazza is the walled **Camposanto** (www.opapisa.it; combined ticket for visiting several Piazza dei Miracoli monuments), a unique 13th-century, cloister-like cemetery filled with sacred soil brought back from the Holy Land.

The walls were once covered with remarkable 14–15th-century frescoes, some of which were created by the renowned artist, Benozzo Gozzoli. However, these were badly damaged during World War II bombing raids and removed to the **Museo delle Sinopie** (www.opapisa.it; combined ticket for Piazza dei Miracoli monuments) in Piazza del Duomo.

The sleek **Museo del Duomo**, reopened after extensive renovations in 2019, is housed in a former 13th-century monastery in the Piazza del Duomo. It shelters a wealth of artwork

Pisa's most famous sight

taken from the Duomo and Baptistery, including breathtaking works by Nicola and Giovanni Pisano.

SIENA

The hilltop city of **Siena** 36, situated approximately 34km (21 miles) south of Florence, has somehow retained its medieval character and charm throughout the centuries. Its walls enclose a fascinating maze of narrow, winding streets that have survived virtually unchanged since the 16th century and earlier. As you make your approach to Siena along a road cut through a succession of undulating hills covered with the region's distinctive rich, reddish-brown soil, you will understand how the colour 'burnt sienna' came by its name.

The city itself is a wonderful marriage of brick and stone, all weathered reds and warm pinks. Imposing Gothic architecture prevails within the city walls, from the main square's early 14th-century Palazzo Pubblico, with its graceful and slender 97m (320ft) tower,

SIENA'S PALIO

If you are in the region over the 2 July or 16 August, it's worth going out of your way to see the Palio, a traditional bareback horse race held in the Piazza del Campo since the 13th century.

After a stately hour-long parade of colourful pages, men-at-arms, knights and flag-twirlers dressed in 15th-century costumes, 10 fiercely competitive bareback riders, each representing a different *contrada* (city ward), battle it out during three wild laps around the dirt-covered piazza. The winning *contrada* is awarded the coveted Palio, a painted silken standard. The only rule is that the riders must not interfere with each other's reins; otherwise, anything goes – and often does.

No tickets are needed for the huge, emotional crowd on the Campo, sweltering in the summer heat. Try to reserve a seat in the stands or a place on a balcony with a view, as the Campo is uncomfortable at best. However, tickets can be virtually impossible to obtain.

the Torre del Mangia, to the grand zebra-striped cathedral and many fine palazzos. Siena truly offers the chance to step back in time.

The view from the Torre del Mangia

Piazza del Campo

The heart of the city is the huge, sloping, fan-shaped **Piazza del Campo** Ⓐ (commonly known as Il Campo), where the Palio horse race (see box) takes place twice each summer. Siena's atmosphere of aristocratic grandeur befits the proud Ghibelline stronghold it once was. According to ancient myth, it was founded by the descendants of Remus (whose twin brother Romulus founded Rome), while in reality it was colonised by the ancient Romans under Augustus. This most stubbornly independent of Tuscan cities remained a republic for over 400 years, until it was defeated by Florence in 1555 and soon thereafter slipped into a centuries-long slumber.

Within the Campo's **Palazzo Pubblico** Ⓑ is the **Museo Civico** (https://museocivico.comune.siena.it; charge), where you can see Siena-born artist Simone Martini's early yet important frescoes of the *Maestà* (Madonna Enthroned; 1315), and the *Condottiere Guidoriccio da Fogliano* (1328) on his richly caparisoned horse. In the adjacent Sala della Pace (Hall of Peace) are Ambrogio Lorenzetti's impressive allegorical frescoes, *The Effect of Good and Bad Government* (1339), among the largest medieval paintings of a secular theme.

San Gimignano, the medieval town of towers

Piazza del Duomo

Almost all of historic Siena is closed to traffic. Wander freely through the picturesque, winding and hilly streets to the great Gothic **Duomo** ⓒ (www.operaduomo.siena.it; combined ticket grants access to the Baptistery, crypt, Piccolomini Library and the adjacent Museo dell'Opera: the Opi Si Pass), perched atop Siena's highest point. Begun in 1196, it is visible from afar for its striking black and white striped exterior, a motif repeated in the city's coat of arms. The attractions within include the uniquely intricate inlaid marble floor, a splendid sculptured octagonal pulpit (1265) by Nicola Pisano, and Pinturicchio's colourful historical frescoes (1509) in the adjoining Piccolomini Library. A viewing balcony, La Porta del Cielo or Gateway to Heaven (guided tours Mar–early Jan; opt for the all-inclusive Porta del Cielo ticket), affords spectacular views into the Duomo's interior and the city itself.

In the neighbouring **Museo dell'Opera del Duomo** (www.operaduomo.siena.it; combined ticket with the cathedral's attractions: the Opa Si Pass), the focal point is the splendid *Maestà* (1308) by local master painter Duccio. He is one of the leading Italian painters of Siena's important 13th- and 14th-century school of art, whose finest examples are on display in the city's art gallery, the **Pinacoteca**

Nazionale (www.pinacotecanazionalesiena.it; charge), housed south of the Duomo in the imposing Palazzo Buonsignori.

SANTA MARIA DELLA SCALA

Opposite the Duomo entrance is the **Santa Maria della Scala** D (www.santamariadellascala.com; closed Tues; charge). In its heyday this former pilgrim's hospital was one of the most important in the world. The vast complex, comprising the hospital and several floors of cellars, now functions as a cultural centre. Highlights are the Sala del Pellegrinaio (ground floor), with stunning frescoes illustrating the story of this hospital, Jacopo della Quercia's original sculpted panels from the Fonte Gaia (Fountain of Joy) in Siena's Campo and the archeological museum.

SAN GIMIGNANO

The town of **San Gimignano** 37 is one of Italy's most evocative. Set on a hilltop, its skyline bristles with the angular outlines of traditional 12–13th-century Tuscan tower-houses. It was a matter of prestige to build the tallest tower possible, so at one point San Gimignano had over 70. Over a dozen remain today.

The 12th-century **Collegiata** church (also called the Duomo, though it is not officially a cathedral; www.duomosangimignano.it; charge), with its plain-facade, is filled with impressive frescoes. The **Cappella di Santa Fina** (1475) is decorated with Ghirlandaio murals that depict San Gimignano's towers in the background. Santa Fina was a local mystic who was adopted as one of the town's patron saints (with San Gimignano).

The 13–14th-century **Palazzo del Popolo** (town hall), with its 54m (177ft) tower, contains San Gimigniano's **Musei Civici** (www.sangimignanomusei.it; charge), with Etruscan and Roman finds, Medieval frescoes and a Pinacoteca (art gallery) reflecting the emergence of the Renaissance. From here, you can wind up the Torre Grossa (included in entry), to admire the panoramic views.

Ponte Vecchio

Things to do

Compact and pedestrian friendly, Florence's historic core was built for walking. Visible from points across town, the famous Duomo – unmatched by any architectural creation in Italy – irresistibly beckons as a first stop, but beyond this big-hitter a wealth of vistas await. On a leisurely stroll you can trace the Arno's banks, enter eye-popping chapels and explore the vast galleries of Renaissance treasures, not least the vast picture collection of the eminent Uffizi. Moving on, indulge in retail therapy and enjoy an evening *aperitivo* in a breezy piazza, or climb (or board a bus) to Fiesole or the Piazzale Michelangelo and San Miniato al Monte for sunset views looking back on Brunelleschi's magnificent dome.

CULTURE

For art-lovers, Florence has no equal in Europe. Every eminent artistic figure from Giotto onwards – Masaccio, Donatello, Botticelli, Leonardo da Vinci, Michelangelo – is represented here, in an unrivalled concentration of churches, galleries and museums. The fabulously decorated chapels of Santa Croce and Santa Maria Novella are forerunners of such astonishing creations as are Masaccio's superb frescoes in the Cappella Brancacci. Throw in Florence's avant-garde Teatro dell'Opera di Firenze (opera house), home to concert halls and an open-air amphitheatre, and the Teatro Verdi for light opera, ballet, jazz and rock concerts – and you can see why the city is a cultural trove.

The avant-garde Teatro dell'Opera di Firenze (opera house) in the Parco della Cascine (Piazzale Vittorio Gui 1) seats 1800, and also has concert halls and an open-air amphitheatre. It is the main venue for Florence's premiere musical institution, Maggio Musicale (see Festivals). Teatro Verdi (Via Ghibellina 99; www.orchestradellatoscana.it) is the venue for light opera, ballet, jazz and rock concerts. Tickets can be booked online.

Summertime alfresco concerts are held in the **Boboli Garden**. Organ recitals are presented in historic churches in September and October, though sporadically in the colder winter months; the churches aren't heated. During June, July and August, nearby **Fiesole** holds the Estate Fiesolana festival of concerts, ballet, drama and film staged at the restored Roman amphitheatre. The opera season gets under way in December and runs until April, held mostly at the Teatro dell'Opera di Firenze. An impressive chamber-music season is run by the **Amici della Musica** (https://amicimusicafirenze.it) in the Teatro della Pergola.

FESTIVALS

Maggio Musicale (www.maggiofiorentino.com): Held from late April to the end of June, this is the highlight of the musical year in Florence, attracting some of the finest concert, ballet and operatic performers in the world. Other noteworthy events include June's **Florence Rocks** (www.firenzerocks.it), one of Italy's largest rock festivals, and the **Florence Biennale** (www.firenzerocks.it), held in the autumn of odd years to celebrate contemporary art and design.

Maggio Musicale Fiorentino Orchestra

NIGHTLIFE

Florence is not renowned for nightclubs, but it has plenty of bars, often with live music and/or an evening buffet for the price of an *aperitivo*. Options include the rowdier pubs and karaoke bars dotting the streets south of Piazza Santa Croce; the bohemian wine bars and microbreweries of Piazza Santo Spirito and the San Niccolò District; and a mounting rank of exclusive, rooftop cocktail bars like Divina Terrazza (www.hotelcavour.com), with stunning Duomo views.

NOTES

For centuries, Florence has been a major centre of hand-printing and bookbinding. In the past few decades these crafts have enjoyed a revival. Shops sell specialised stationery and items such as notebooks, frames and albums covered in handmade marbled paper. Beautifully crafted creations include leather-bound books such as diaries, address books and journals.

SHOPPING

WHERE TO SHOP

A fashion locus, Florence's old centre is packed with dressed shop windows competing for your attention, most famously along the expensive Via dei Tornabuoni, location of Gucci, Tod's, Ferragamo and Dolce & Gabbana. The Florentine house of Emilio Pucci, with bold brightly coloured prints that evoke the 1960s, can be found on Via dei Tornabuoni 20–22r. Other good nearby hunting grounds are the Via della Vigna Nuova, the Via del Parione and Via Strozzi. Ferragamo fans should not miss the engaging shoe museum in the basement of the Ferragamo flagship store, Via dei Tornabuoni 4r–14r, while Gucci enthusiasts can visit the Gucci Garden in Piazza Signoria which tells the story of the designer and displays original pieces.

San Lorenzo's famous market is awash with good-value leather stalls that sell everything from handbags and luggage to wallets and gloves. For top of the range quality and prices you should start

FLORENTINE MARKETS

The biggest and most popular market is **San Lorenzo**, which caters to both tourists and locals, and sells everything from football banners to sunglasses. You will find clothing (T-shirts, knitwear and woollen scarves), shoes and leatherwear, often at reasonable prices, but don't expect high-quality goods.

At its centre, stretching along Via dell' Ariento, is the late 19th-century structure that houses the **Mercato Centrale**, the city's largest and most colourful food market, bulging at the seams with just about everything produced in the surrounding Tuscan hills, from fresh fruit and vegetables to meat, fish and game. It is a great place for local colour, photo opportunities, insight into Florentine daily life and culinary heritage.

The **Mercato Nuovo**, or **Straw Market**, is conveniently located halfway between the Duomo and the Ponte Vecchio. Housed beneath a 16th-century loggia, a score of stalls sell leather bags and other miscellaneous souvenirs – a far less expansive (and less interesting) selection than its big-sister market at San Lorenzo.

A daily **flea market** operates in Piazza dei Ciompi, selling the usual mix of junk and bric-a-brac found in flea markets the world over. A more genuine antiques market is also held in the same spot, and takes place on the last Sunday of each month.

Sant'Ambrogio morning market in Piazza Ghiberti sells fresh foodstuffs, including pasta, porcini mushrooms and other Italian specialities.

A huge weekly market every Tuesday morning in **Cascine Park** sells all kinds of goods to a far less touristy clientele (little English is spoken). This market is especially good for buying cheap clothes and shoes, or live chickens, whose days are numbered.

with the designer boutiques in the Via de'Tornabuoni or the shops in streets around the Piazza della Repubblica. The Santa Croce leather school (Scuola dei Cuoio; http://leatherschool.biz) inside the monastery of Santa Croce, is a popular place to watch skilled Florentine leather-workers and to purchase their creations.

Antiques are clustered around two main areas: Via Maggio and the surrounding streets in the Oltrarno and Borgo Ognissanti, west of the centre. For framed, vintage prints, head to the **Piazza del Duomo**; for unframed prints, try the **San Lorenzo market.**

For hand-painted ceramics, Sbigoli Terrecotte (Via Sant'Egidio 4r) has a good choice of beautiful Tuscan plates, cups and trays, with both traditional and contemporary designs.

For gold and silver, the ultimate place to window shop is along the **Ponte Vecchio**, a bridge lined with dazzling, centuries-old jewellers' shops, each window more tempting (and densely stocked) than the last. Prices are not for the faint-hearted.

As for inlay and mosaic work, find both modern interpretations and replicas of classic patterns for sale in **Lungarno Torrigiani, Via Guicciardini** and **Piazza Santa Croce**.

A jewellery shop on Ponte Vecchio

Tourist and souvenir **markets** are held daily in the sprawling San Lorenzo area, and the less expansive Mercato Nuovo; the local market held every Tuesday morning in Cascine Park is the largest in Florence, selling everything from wine and cheese to clothes and shoes.

WHAT TO BUY

Since the Middle Ages, Florentines have held craftsmanship in high regard, and the city's elegant shops are famed for the quality of their merchandise, especially

NOTES

Shops traditionally close for a long lunch break (1/1.30–3.30/4pm), but an increasing number are open all day. Many shops don't open on Sunday or operate reduced hours, while some shops close on Monday morning. Many shops close for 7–10 days (minimum) on and around the 15 August for Ferragosto (Assumption Day). Shops may hang a sign reading '*chiuso per ferie*' (closed for vacation).

fashion and leather goods. Some of Italy's best designers started out in Florence, with many flagship stores still found in the city.

Florence has been known for its quality **leather goods** since the Middle Ages. This is the hometown of the shoe and bag making greats Ferragamo and Gucci. The best buys in town are shoes and small leather goods: gloves, belts, purses, wallets and boxes, in all shapes and sizes and of varying quality. Handbags and outerwear can be gorgeous and tempting but do not expect bargains.

Also prized are **antiques**. Look out for old picture frames, jewellery, ceramics, statues, paintings and furniture; however you are unlikely to find a bargain. Better value is often found in framed 18th-century prints of Florence. Regional **ceramic** specialities include expensive, high-quality table china and brightly hand-painted ceramics of centuries-old Tuscan patterns and colours.

Designer **gold jewellery** is expensive (and almost always 18-carat), and most of it is now made in Arezzo. Every piece should be stamped, confirming that it is solid gold (ask to see the stamp, as minuscule as it may be). The work of Florence's unsung silversmiths is invariably beautiful and practical. Look for pillboxes, napkin rings, photo frames, cruet sets, sugar bowls and candlesticks.

The Florentine speciality of *intarsio*, the art of wood or semi-precious stone **inlay**, was perfected during the Renaissance. Some examples can be seen in the Uffizi, but the craft still flourishes.

Larger items such as tabletops are inevitably expensive and exorbitant to ship; small, framed 'naïve' pictures of birds, flowers, Tuscan landscapes or views of Florence are much less prohibitive.

Florence also boasts some of the most alluring fragrances in the form of locally made **soaps** and **perfumes**. One of the world's oldest apothecaries is here: The **Officina Profumo Farmaceutica di Santa Maria Novella** (Via della Scala 16; https://eu.smnovella.com), where Dominican monks have concocted herbal medicines for centuries, having once received the generous patronage of Catherine de' Medici.

OUTDOOR ACTIVITIES

Boating. For a seldom-seen perspective of the city, glide beneath Florence's bridges on a traditional, shallow-bottom *barchetto*. Tours by I Renaioli (www.renaioli.it) are available between May and September, lasting around 45 minutes.

Cycling. A national sport, as well as a great way to get around town. There are delightful rides in the surrounding countryside, too. Bikes are easy to hire (see page 126). Cycling routes and maps are available from the tourist bureau's website (www.feelflorence.it). Florence Town (www.florencetown.com) offers two-and-a-half-hour guided bike

Men's handmade shoes

A fruit and vegetable stall at Mercato Centrale

tours, from April to October daily at 10am (also at 3pm), meeting in Piazza Mentana. You can also take advantage of Ridemovi's bike-sharing system (now with e-bikes available too) by downloading the app at www.ridemovi.com.

Football. If cycling is a national sport then football *(calcio)* is a national passion. The local team is Fiorentina (www.acffiorentina.com). They play in Serie A at the Stadio Artemio Franchi near the Campo di Marte railway station. If you are in Florence on or around the feast of St John (late June), you may want to catch the Calcio in Costume, where a rough-and-tumble medieval version of the game is played in period costume.

Walking. There are endless options for great walks in the rolling green hills that surround the city. Visit Bellosguardo, Fiesole, the Certosa del Galluzzo monastery, Poggio Imperiale or the Arcetri observatory, set on the hill where Galileo gazed at the stars. All are within easy reach of the city, but you will certainly feel like you are in the Tuscan countryside. The tourist bureau's website (www.feel-florence.it) has a number of useful walking maps of the province. More ambitious walkers can consider the long-distance **Via degli Dei** (Way of Gods; https://en.viadeglidei.it), linking Florence with Bologna; and the Camino di Dante (Dante's Route; www.ilcamminodidante.it), linking Florence to Ravenna, where the poet was laid to rest.

FLORENCE FOR CHILDREN

Young children quickly tire of visiting museums and galleries, especially in the heat of summer. To keep things running smoothly, intersperse museum visits with ice cream from the city's many *gelaterie*, or visit the pigeons and cart horses that congregate in the Piazza della Signoria. The Boboli and Bardini Gardens and the Cascine are Florence's main parks, where children can let off steam.

Older children might enjoy the climb to the top of the campanile or the dome in the cathedral, if they can tolerate over 400 steps each. Consider a visit to one of the more offbeat museums run by the University

NOTES

Housed in the Palazzo Strozzino (kitty-corner from the Palazzo Strozzi), the Giunti Odeon (www.giuntiodeon.com) is far more than its attractive patisserie and café. A delight for bibliophiles and cinephiles alike, it's a fully-fledged bookstore and cinema making the most of the same airy, elegant space. The creative, multi-use format – offering a welcome rest from sightseeing, whether to peruse new titles or enjoy movie snacks from the seating on the mezzanine floor – was unveiled in 2023. The Odeon theatre, however, has been synonymous with cinema in Florence since 1922. For evening screening times, check the website.

Children will enjoy climbing up the Campanile

Museum System (www.sma.unifi.it). These include the 'Specola' **Natural History Museum** in the Oltrarno district, the **Anthropology and Ethnology Museum** just south of the Duomo and the **Museum of Geology and Palaeontology** immediately east of San Marco. The **Stibbert Museum** (www.museostibbert.it) is a little out of town, but the superb armour collections will spark their imaginations.

The Associazione MUS.E (https://musefirenze.it) puts on a host of well-organised activities for children on a reservation-only basis at several of Florence's museums, including Palazzo Vecchio and the Museo Novecento. Activities include the 'Secret Passages' tours (*Percorsi Segreti*; daily at various times), which take in secret passages and odd corners made for the rulers, or the 'Life at Court' tours (*Vita di Corte*; weekends) including an opportunity for children to wear 16th-century clothes and play with princes' toys.

CALENDAR OF EVENTS

February/March Shrove Tuesday: a low-key event in Florence, but nearby villages celebrate with fireworks and processions.

25 March Annunciation Day: celebrated with a small fair in Piazza della Santissima Annunziata.

March/April Easter Sunday Scoppio del Carro (Explosion of the Cart): In Piazza del Duomo an ox-drawn cart full of fireworks is set off by a mechanical dove that travels by wire from the cathedral's high altar at midday mass.

23 May Ascension Day, Festa del Grillo (Festival of the Cricket): fair in Cascine Park popular with children. Crickets in cages sold to be set free.

Late April to late June Maggio Musicale (Musical May; www.maggiofiorentino.com): prestigious programme of opera, ballet and concerts throughout the city by local and visiting artists.

16–17 June San Ranieri Historical Regatta, Pisa. The city's patron saint is celebrated by illuminations, processions and races along the river.

Last Sunday in June Il Gioco del Ponte, Pisa. Twelve teams take part in a tug-of-war on the Ponte di Mezzo across the Arno.

June to August Estate Fiesolana: summer festival of music, ballet and theatre in the hilltop town of Fiesole.

24 June Feast of St John the Baptist, patron saint of Florence, celebrated with fireworks. Calcio in Costume: historical rowdy football game in 16th-century costume in Piazza Santa Croce, preceded by a parade.

2 July and 16 August Palio di Siena: historic pageant and raucous horse race in Siena's beautiful Piazza del Campo.

10 August Festa di San Lorenzo: an outdoor celebration in Piazza San Lorenzo with live music and free lasagna and watermelon.

7 September Festa della Rificolona (Festival of the Chinese Lanterns): procession with paper lanterns, Ponte San Niccolò.

September to December Main opera season, with performances at the Teatro dell'Opera di Firenze, Piazzale Vittorio Gui 1.

Food and drink

Tuscan food has long dominated Florence's restaurant scene, with an emphasis on straightforward, simply prepared *cucina povera* ('poor man's fare'): few seasonings, no elaborate sauces and the full flavour of primary ingredients. Indeed, your first taste of traditional crusty Tuscan bread, a staple at every meal, will immediately tell you that it contains no salt (and is not eaten with butter), a tradition persisting from the Middle Ages, when salt was a luxury item. Tuscan olive oil, another staple, is commonly extra virgin and is widely regarded as the finest in the world – dark green in colour, with a rich, peppery flavour. Tuscan olive oil is used in varying degrees on everything from soup to salad.

But while Tuscan *trattorie, osterie, enoteche* – and, increasingly, *paninoteche* (sandwich shops) – remain amply represented, the restaurant scene has branched in various directions with twists on old traditions. To widely varying degrees of success, some have chased the vicissitudes of TikTok trends (often easily spotted thanks to block-length lines) while others have innovated with seasonal and locally sourced ingredients. Florence's line-up has also come to include cuisines from the Caucasus, South Asia, the Middle East and Japan. While in Florence, however, you shouldn't pass up the chance to sample a few of the old Tuscan favourites, from *pappardelle al cinghiale* (wild boar ragù) to *pappa al pomodoro* (tomato soup) to a *panino con lampredotto* (don't ask, just enjoy!).

TOP 10 THINGS TO TRY

1. TUSCAN PASTA AND PIZZA

Two popular typically Tuscan pastas are *pappardelle alla lepre* (broad noodles, usually home-made, with a tomato-based sauce of wild hare) and *strozzapreti* (a 'priest strangler' of pasta, cheese and spinach, usually baked in the oven and dressed in a simple tomato

Pappardelle alla lepre

sauce). Some restaurants will serve half portions (*mezza porzione*) of pasta upon request. The Neapolitan pizzas at Il Pizzaiuolo are among the best in the city (there are 30 great value varieties on offer), and the rest of the menu has a Neapolitan touch too – as does the atmosphere, which is high-spirited.

2. ANTIPASTI

Antipasti are staples across Italy, such as *antipasto misto* (a mixed spread of starters) and *melone con prosciutto* (cantaloupe with cured ham). Look out for Tuscan specialities such as *prosciutto con fichi* (prosciutto with fresh figs), Tuscan *crostini* (toast-rounds topped with chopped chicken livers, anchovies, capers, etc), or *fet-tunta* (toasted country bread rubbed with garlic and drizzled with olive oil). This is unfussy farmer's fare that rarely disappoints.

3. LOCAL DELI PRODUCTS

Delicious local deli foods not to miss out on include *finocchiona*, Tuscany's fennel-studded salami, and the wide range of Italian hams, *mortadella*, sausages and other cold meats. Cheese is also an Italian staple; varieties you should try include *stracchino*, *pecorino* (a tangy sheep's-milk cheese), ricotta, *provola* (smoked or fresh), *gorgonzola*, *parmigiano* and *grana*.

4. TUSCAN BAKED GOODS

With so much to choose from, it's possible to find yourself in a conundrum of where to find the best baked goods in Florence. Albeit the tiny size, this city is brimming with pastry shops (*la pasticceria*) and bakery shops (*il forno*) luring you in with wafts of sweet and savoury temptations. Some of the most popular Tuscan bakes include: *la schiacciata*, considered the Tuscan focaccia; *coccoli*, little fried doughballs traditionally stuffed with cream cheese and ham; *fedora*, a moist sponge cake with a thick layer of whipped cream and dark chocolate, flavoured with orange essence; *sfogliatina*, a puff-pastry pocket sometimes filled with cream custard, ricotta and pear – and if made right, the sugar and fat have a slight caramelised crisp at the ends of the pastry.

Bruschetta

5. TUSCAN SOUPS

Though often overlooked, there is nothing better than a hearty, flavoursome Tuscan soup on a chilly day. Among the most popular in Florence are *pappa al pomodoro* (tomato soup thickened with bread), *ribollita* (a filling 'twice boiled' bread-based vegetable soup), and the staple *minestra* (a seasonal mixed vegetable soup, sometimes with pasta; variations on this are found throughout Italy).

6. BISTECCA ALLA FIORENTINA

A long-time favourite in Florence is the *bistecca alla fiorentina* – a huge, charcoal-grilled T-bone steak, served with lemon or drizzled with olive oil. Each steak is at least 4cm (about 1.5in) thick and weighs 1.2–1.5kg (42–53oz). They are traditionally cooked to be charred and crispy on the outside, while remaining rare and tender on the inside. Diners should be aware that steak is sold by the weight and is not cheap. Unless you've skipped lunch, plan to split with a partner to avoid any waste.

7. MERCATO CENTRALE LUNCH

At Florence's centre is the late 19th-century structure that houses the iconic Mercato Centrale – a lunch spot that everyone should experience. The city's largest and most colourful food market, Mercato Centrale bulges at the seams with just about every fresh foodstuff produced in Tuscany – from fruit, vegetables, meat, fish and game to other Italian specialities. It is a great place for an insight into Florentine daily life and culinary heritage. But even better, the upper level has an indoor piazza with bars and eateries, which deliver simple local cuisine utilising the fresh produce available to them.

8. TRIPPA ALLA FIORENTINA

A Florentine street food staple, *trippa alla fiorentina* (stewed tripe) is made with strips of tripe that are simmered with onions, carrots, celery, hot peppers and tomatoes. Once fully cooked and tender, it is served drizzled with Tuscan olive oil and sprinkled with grated parmigiano cheese. When reheated the next day, it's said that *trippa alla fiorentina* tastes even better. The dish is commonly flavoured with bay leaves, but sweet basil leaves are also often added, especially during the summer. It's recommended to accompany *trippa alla fiorentina* with a few slices of Tuscan bread.

9. TUSCAN WINES

For many, Italian wine is Chianti – a basic pressing made from the Sangiovese grape. After a brief period of dormancy, Chianti production has experienced a resurgence of popularity and sales, and is once again considered one of Europe's premier wines. The official Consortium-designated Chianti region stretches from Florence to Siena, entitling producers within the region to bear the Gallo Nero (black rooster) seal. Those with a gold border indicate a Chianti Classico Riserva, meaning it was aged a year longer before bottling. Tuscany produces a number of other superior reds, including Brolio, Vino Nobile di Montepulciano and the fine aged Brunello di Montalcino. Tuscan whites are unremarkable apart from the dry and elegant Vernaccia di San Gimignano.

Traditional ice cream shop in Florence

10. GELATO

Desserts do not generally hold the same importance in Italy as they do in some countries, however, an exception is always made for *gelato*. Italian ice cream is generally of a very high quality – Italians would rather pay more and eat something made with fresh ingredients. A basic ice cream is usually made with milk, cream, eggs and sugar, and the tastes are strikingly pure. A bewildering choice of delicious ice creams can be found in the city's many *gelaterie* – the best serve fruit varieties made from whatever fruits are in season.

NOTES

Italian cooking is essentially regional. Each of the country's 20 regions has its own unique specialities rarely found outside its boundaries, and similar dishes may have different names from region to region.

WHERE TO EAT

The streets of Florence's historic centre are packed with cafés and bars where you can buy a beverage, snack or quick lunch to enjoy while standing at the bar or seated, or to take away. Sitting at a table will cost more, while sitting outside can be twice, or even three times, as expensive. Another option is the *tavola calda* (hot table), a self-service café where you can choose from a selection of pre-prepared dishes. These alternatives can be good for lunch, but those that cater to tourists usually offer mediocre, though often convenient, meals.

Restaurants range from an expensive *ristorante* to a slightly more modestly priced family *trattoria*. Generally speaking, the further away from the tourist attractions you go, the less expensive and less touristy the restaurants become. Reservations are recommended for more expensive establishments. Many restaurants still include a cover charge *(coperto)* and some a service *(servizio)* charge of 10–15 percent. If not, leave 10–15 percent for the waiter.

Chefs preparing home-made pasta

As in the rest of Italy, restaurants tend to offer four main courses. The meal may start with an *aperitivo* (a drink accompanied by nibbles, such as olives) or *antipasto* (slightly heavier appetiser, such as a platter of cold meats). The first course is known as the *primo* (often soup, pasta and, occasionally, risotto), followed by the *secondo* (main course of meat, game or fish, usually grilled or (optional side dishes) are ordered separately and arrive with the entrée.

WHEN TO EAT

Breakfast *(prima colazione)* is usually included in the price of accommodation, and most hotels offers a buffet with rolls, fresh fruit, yogurt, cereal, homemade pastries, juice and coffee. Breakfast is usually served 7.30–10am.

Lunch *(pranzo, or colazione)* is served 12.30–2.30pm, though a limited number of places in Florence's centre will serve food throughout the entire afternoon. Cafés will always provide something to fill the gaps for a mid-afternoon snack *(merenda)*. Alternatively, wait until around 7pm to enjoy an *aperitivo*: a beverage with light accompanying snacks that act as a warm-up for the evening meal.

Dinner *(cena)* begins at around 7.30pm and typically stretches for at least an hour. While traditionally a fully-fledged affair of four courses, this is increasingly only the case on special occasions. It's completely acceptable to opt for a lighter meal (an appetizer plus one *primo* or *secondo*, for example), which incidentally will increase your chances of retaining leftover room for *gelato* later.

WHAT TO DRINK

Thirst-quenchers range from Chianti wine to Italian beer *(birra)*, summertime iced tea – peach- or lemon-flavoured *(tè freddo alla*

PICNICS

For a breath of air, make up a picnic lunch and head for the hills of Fiesole, the Boboli or Bardini Gardens, or the terrace of San Miniato al Monte in the area of Piazzale Michelangelo. The central square providing the most shade is Santo Spirito, near the Pitti Palace. Buy fresh fruit and bread from the market, then find one of the many Florentine delicatessens *(pizzicheria or salumeria)* or small grocers *(alimentari)* who stock a wide range of food and drink (including mineral water and soft drinks), and often sell sandwich rolls *(panini)*.

Delicious foods to try include *finocchiona*, Tuscany's fennel-studded salami, and the wide range of Italian hams, salamis, *mortadella*, sausages and other cold meats. Cheese is also an important Italian picnic ingredient. Varieties to try include *stracchino, pecorino* (a tangy sheep's-milk cheese), *ricotta, provola* (smoked or fresh), *gorgonzola, parmigiano* and *grana*.

Diners at Piazza della Signoria

pesca or al limone), a non-alcoholic bitter *(amaro)*, freshly squeezed fruit juice *(spremuta)*, iced espresso *(caffè freddo)*, orangeade or lemonade *(aranciata or limonata)*. There is always the alternative of mineral water *(acqua minerale)*, still or carbonated *(naturale or gasata)*. Florence's tap water is heavily chlorinated, but is safe to drink, albeit a little unpleasant.

End your meal with a small glass of *vin santo* (holy wine), a deep amber-coloured sweet wine, or choose from a local *grappa* (a distillate of grape must) or *limoncello*, a lemon-infused vodka served ice-cold.

An after-meal **espresso** *(un caffè)* is also available in decaffeinated form *(decaffinato)*. You can order it short, long, *macchiato* ('stained' with a dot of steamed milk) or just *normale*, black. Ordering a *cappuccino* after 11am marks you as a tourist, but waiters are accustomed to the request of after-dinner cappuccinos by now (ordering coffee together with your dinner remains taboo). For a greater ratio of water with your coffee, order a *caffè americano*.

While coffee tends to be the most popular choice of hot drink among Italians, you may be able to order a cup of tea in some eating and drinking establishments as well as in hotels, although it's less common. For those with a sweet tooth, you can't skip an Italian hot chocolate *(cioccolato cialdo)*; rich, thick and delicious.

TO HELP YOU ORDER...

A table for one/two/three please **Un tavolo per una persona/ per due/per tre**

I would like... **Vorrei...**

The bill please **Il conto per favore**

What would you recommend? **Cosa ci consiglia?**

I don't eat meat **No mangio carne**

...AND READ THE MENU

aglio garlic
agnello lamb
aragosta lobster
basilica basil
birra beer
bistecca beefsteak
burro butter
calamari squid
carciofi artichokes
cavallo horse
cinghiale wild boar
cipolle onions
coniglio rabbit
cozze mussels
fagioli beans
finocchio fennel
formaggio cheese
frutti di mare seafood
funghi mushrooms
gamberetti shrimps
gamberi prawns
gelato ice cream
insalata salad
lumache snails
maiale pork
manzo beef
melanzane aubergine
olio oil
olive olives
pane bread
panna cream
patate potatoes
peperoni peppers
pesce fish
pollo chicken
polpo/pólipo octopus
pomodori tomatoes
prosciutto ham
riso rice
salsiccie sausages
spinaci spinach
tonno tuna
uova eggs
verdure vegetables
vino wine
vitello veal
vongole clams
zuppa soup

Places to eat

As a basic guide, we have used the following symbols to give an indication of the price of a three-course meal per person, excluding wine.
€€€€ = over 80 euros
€€€ = 50–80 euros
€€ = 25–50 euros
€ = below 25 euros

CENTRO STORICO (CENTRE)

RESTAURANTS

Frescobaldi Piazza della Signoria 31, www.frescobaldifirenze.it. Serving regional classics like *pappardelle al cinghiale* (wild boar ragù), all paired with excellent wines from the Frescobaldi family's vineyards. Choose between an elegant interior with whitewashed vaulting offset by gorgeous tiles or piazza seating with views of the Palazzo Vecchio. **€€€**

Gustavino Via della Condotta 37r, https://gustavino.it. The Tuscan cuisine here is creative without being too elaborate or over fussy, and is beautifully served in a warm, cosy space. Look out for the speciality wine-and-food evenings they run. Great pizza too. **€€€**

Ora d'Aria Via dei Georgofili 11r, www.oradariaristorante.com. Very handy for the Uffizi, this chic and highly popular little restaurant is renowned for light contemporary variations on classic Tuscan fare. Expect dishes such as macaroni soufflé, urchin risotto, broad bean soup with roast squid and steak tartare served with diced pear. Reservations recommended. Closed Sun. **€€€**

La Prosciutteria Via de' Neri, 54r, www.laprosciutteria.com. For an inexpensive lunch, head to this busy, rustic *neo-vinaio*, serving big platters of cold meats and cheese along with home-baked *schiacciate* to accompany the good-value wine. **€**

Il Vegetariano Via delle Ruote 30r, https://il-vegetariano.com. Florence, home of *bistecca alla fiorentina*, has few vegetarian restaurants, but this is certainly one of the best. It is cafeteria-style and crowded but is worth persevering with for the daily-changing dishes (both vegetarian and vegan), made with the freshest of vegetables. Interesting salads too – and all at very affordable prices. Closed for dinner Mon, closed for lunch Sat and Sun. **€**

CAFÉS AND BARS

Caffè Gilli Piazza della Repubblica 39r, www.caffegilli.com. Founded over 250 years ago, Caffè Gilli is the plushest of all the cafés on the Piazza Repubblica. The café is redolent of a bygone era (particularly the old-fashioned interior), with its silver service and impeccable waiters. A traditional favourite place to rendezvous, it is famous for its chocolates and especially its *gianduja*. **Caffè Paszkowski** (www.caffepaszkowski.com; next door) is known for its summer evenings with live music. **€€**

Caffè Rivoire Piazza della Signoria 4r, https://rivoire.it. This is arguably the most famous of all of Florence's historic cafés. It has a ringside seat in Florence's most picturesque piazza, overlooking Michelangelo's *David*. Outside seating is perfect for iced tea, light lunch and people watching. Thick, dark hot chocolate is a local wintertime tradition. Activity flutters around the bar; proper service at the inside tables attracts society ladies of a certain age, along with foot-weary tourists. **€€**

Caffè Scudieri Piazza di San Giovanni 19r, www.scudieri.it. Elegant café with somewhat pricey coffee and treats (and a decent dinner menu too), though more than reasonable considering the enviable location, immediately opposite the baptistery, with an enticing sliver of the Santa Maria del Fiore in view around the bend – an excellent spot for people watching right at the heart of Florence's old core. **€€**

Cantinetta del Verrazzano Via dei Tavolini 18r, www.verrazzano.com. Popular, good-value wine bar serving wines from the family vineyards in Chianti's Castello di Verrazzano. Baked breads from the wood-burning ovens make this a great place to stop for a *merenda* (snack) or light meal, with a dozen Tuscan wines by the glass. **€€**

Enoteca Bacarossa Vicolo dei Gondi 3r, www.facebook.com/EnotecaBaccaRossa. Tucked away down a side alley near the Piazza della Signoria, this hidden *enoteca* is among Florence's newest (launched in 2024), with friendly and highly knowledgeable staff and an excellent selection of Tuscan wines. **€**

SANTA CROCE (EAST)

RESTAURANTS

Acqua al Due Via della Vigna Vecchia 40r, www.acquaal2florence.com. Welcoming restaurant and bar behind the Bargello known for its pasta and salad samplers as well as its balsamic – and surprisingly delicious – blueberry steaks. Locals, tourists, students and families share communal tables beneath walls decked with autographed plates. Closed for lunch Mon. **€€**

Il Cibrèo Trattoria Via dei Macci 122r, tel: 055-234 1100. Simple, trattoria-style restaurant that adopts a modern approach to classic Florentine dishes (i.e. no pasta) – *pappa al pomodoro* (a thick garlic-flavoured soup of bread and tomato), *piccione farcito con mostarda di frutta* (pigeon stuffed with spiced fruit), *palombo giovane alla livornese* (Livorno-style dove). Excellent desserts. The adjacent Cibrèo restaurant is widely acclaimed. It shares the same kitchen, but is far more expensive and formal and requires reservations, often far in advance. **€€**

Enoteca Pinchiori Via Ghibellina 87, www.enotecapinchiorri.it. The only restaurant in Tuscany to boast three Michelin stars, this is among the best and most famous restaurants in all of Italy, with one of the world's greatest wine cellars. The menu blends French and Tuscan influences. Think sparkling chandeliers, silver cloches and impeccable service. Formal dress. **€€€€**

Finisterrae Piazza Santa Croce 12, www.finisterraefirenze.com. A Mediterranean bar and restaurant with a selection of food from various cuisines. Start with tapas, followed by a Moroccan-style tagine or pasta dish. The ambience is relaxed and sultry, especially in the bar area. Prices vary depending on the choice of menu. **€€–€€€**

Il Pizzaiuolo Via dei Macci 113r, www.ilpizzaiuolo.it. Reservations are necessary at this hopping pizzeria. A Neapolitan *pizzaiuolo* reigns over the wood-burning oven, turning out thick chewy-crusted pizza. Closed Sun and August. **€**

SAN LORENZO AND SAN MARCO (NORTH)

RESTAURANTS

Zà Zà Piazza Mercato Centrale 26r, www.trattoriazaza.it. Traditional Tuscan fare served at communal wooden tables frequented by tourists, market vendors and shoppers alike. Try the *crostini misti, ribollita* or the famous *bistecca*. **€€**

SANTA MARIA NOVELLA (WEST)

RESTAURANTS

Buca Lapi Via del Trebbio 1r, www.bucalapi.com. In the cellar of the Palazzo Antinori, this charming restaurant serves top-notch *bistecca alla* *fiorentina* (enormous and beautifully grilled). As expected, being in the basement of the palazzo of one of Tuscany's best wine producers, it has an excellent range of wines. Dinner only; closed Sun. **€€€**

Coco Lezzone Via del Parioncino 26/r, https://cocolezzone.it. Small, no-frills institution off the shopping strip Via Tornabuoni, serving classic Florentine food. Try the tasty pasta with porcini mushrooms. Closed Sun and Tues evening. **€€**

Sostanza Via della Porcellana 25r, tel: 055-212 691. Established in 1869, this casual trattoria near Piazza Santa Maria Novella offers minestrone, tripe, fried chicken and *stracotto*, but most people come for the acclaimed Ferragamo *fiorentina* (after all, this place originated as a butcher's shop). Don't miss the *frittata di carciofi* (artichoke omelette) in season. No credit cards. Closed Sun. **€€**

OLTRARNO (SOUTH)

RESTAURANTS

Antica Mescita San Niccolò Via di San Niccolò 60r, tel: 055-234 2836. This *osteria* in Oltrarno does simple and cheap, but extremely good Italian food served up in a cheery, crowded atmosphere. Part of the eatery is set in a former chapel. **€**

Borgo Antico Piazza Santo Spirito 6r, www.borgoanticofirenze.com. Jam-packed trattoria known for great thin-crusted pizzas in a lively, youthful atmosphere. There is a full menu as well, but grab a coveted outdoor piazza table and stick with a simple pizza, salad and carafe of house wine. **€€**

Napoleone Piazza del Carmine 24, www.trattorianapoleone.it. This colourful trattoria, with a quirky interior, is set in a quiet location near the church with a large terrace for summer dining. The regularly changing menu features Tuscan antipasti, champagne risotto, and plates of *salumi* and *bistecca alla fiorentina*. Closed for lunch except on Sun. **€€**

Osteria del Cinghiale Bianco Borgo S. Jacopo 43r, https://cinghiale bianco.com. Traditional dishes including hard-to-find *cinghiale* (wild boar) are even tastier in the medieval, mood-setting ambience accented by a few romantic niche tables. If *cinghiale* is not for you, there is a wide selection of simple classic Tuscan fare. **€€**

Pitti Gola e Cantina Piazza de' Pitti 16, www.pittigolaecantina.com. Fabulous little *enoteca* just opposite Pitti Palace, lined with shelving containing innumerable bottles of wine, many available by the glass. Pasta dishes and simple but tasty plates of *salumi* and cheese help the wine slip down. Closed Tues. **€**

Quattro Leoni Via de' Vellutini 1r, www.4leoni.it. One of the city's oldest restaurants, founded in 1550, the Four Lions is set in the tiny Piazza della Passera where diners can sit outside in summer. The fabulous signature dish is a pear and ricotta pasta in a creamy taleggio sauce. **€€**

San Niccolò Bistrot Via di San Niccolò 39r, tel: 055-200 1397. *San Niccolò* is an elegant take on modern Mediterranean cuisine. The menu offers a seasonal selection of typical ingredients, frequently from the southern regions of Italy, including different kinds of *carpaccio*, salads, soups and pastas. The perfect glass of wine is proposed here to accompany each dish. There is a small outdoor area for the summer. **€€€**

BARS

Le Volpi e l'Uva Piazza dei Rossi 1, www.levolpieluva.com. This superb little wine bar has a fantastic selection of Italian wines, including quite a number of little-known vintages. It also serves very tasty plates of cheese and *salumi*, as well as *schiacciatine* (thin flat bread). **€**

Travel essentials

PRACTICAL INFORMATION

ACCESSIBLE TRAVEL

Florence has made strides in increasing the accessibility of its historic centre, earning commendation in 2021 by the European Network for Accessible Tourism. Still, while many of the more popular attractions are equipped with ramps for wheelchair access, challenges remain, particularly at minor attractions. Unaccompanied visitors will usually experience some difficulty, so it is best to travel with a companion. Specialised tour operators or travel agencies offering customised tours and itineraries for people with disabilities include Sage Traveling (www.sagetraveling.com). In the UK you can obtain further information from Disability Rights UK (www.disabilityrightsuk.org) and in the US from SATH (https://sath.org).

Those with a disabled symbol can obtain free entrance to the city centre limited zone (ZTL). Feel Florence (www.feelflorence.it), the city's official tourism bureau, offers an excellent list of tools and itineraries for those with reduced mobility. At certain sites, such travellers are entitled – along with one companion – free entry plus permission to jump the queue (at Santa Croce and San Lorenzo, for example). Other attractions, such as Brunelleschi's Dome and Giotto's Belltower, remain inaccessible to those with reduced mobility.

ACCOMMODATION

Florence offers a wide range of accommodation, from grand city palazzos and chic boutique hotels to B&Bs and pensione-style hotels. Private home stays are a fairly recent development in Florence but are a good way of experiencing closer contact with the locals while paying modest prices. Serviced apartments, or residences, are an attractive alternative to hotels. The Florence tourist board website (www.feelflorence.it) offers a wide array of accommodation. During the high season between March and October and at Easter and Christmas, Florence becomes very crowded, and accommodation is at a premium. Book as far in advance as possible for these periods. Hotels are graded from one to five stars, but the star system reflects the extent of their facilities, rather than other qualities such as atmosphere, comfort or location.

If you find yourself in Florence without a hotel reservation, head for the tourist information/hotel reservation office opposite the Santa Maria Novella railway station, just behind the church of the same name (tel: 055-000; Mon–Sat 9am–7pm, Sun 9am–5.30pm); they will find you a room within your price range for a small fee.

Florence is expensive, on par at least with the major European cities. Since 2011, a nightly tax on tourists *(tassa di soggiorno)* has been levied according to a hotel's star-rating. This currently starts at €3.50 for one-star lodgings, rising to €8 for a five-star hotel. A €5.50 surcharge is added to all Airbnb bookings. The cheapest hotels tend to be situated around the Santa Maria Novella station area and the most expensive along the banks of the Arno. Breakfast is almost always included in the room rate, varying from an abundant buffet to just rolls and coffee.

Visitors should also consider staying just outside the city, in one of the country villas, or opting for the increasingly popular agriturismo – farm-stay holidays, which are often self-catering.

Do you have any vacancies? **Avete camere libere?**
I'd like a single/double room **Vorrei una camera singola/ matrimoniale**
...with bath/shower/ private toilet **...con bagno/doccia/ gabinetto privato**
What's the rate per night/week? **Qual è il prezzo per una notte/una settimana?**

AIRPORTS

The largest international airport near Florence is the **Aeroporto Galileo Galilei** (www.pisa-airport.com) at Pisa, 85km (52 miles) west of Florence. British Airways (wwwbritishairways.com) flies there from London Heathrow. The budget airline easyJet (www.easyjet.com) flies direct to Pisa from Gatwick, Southend, Luton, Bristol and Manchester while Ryanair (www. ryanair.com) has a regular service from London Stansted and Manchester.

A regular train service (www.trenitalia.com) links Florence to Pisa Centrale station, which can be reached from the airport by train (from platform 14), bus, taxi or a 20-minute walk (1.5km). Alternatively, take one of the coaches (www.caronnatour.com) that run directly between Pisa Airport and Florence SMN station (1hr).

Florence's small but growing airport, **Aeroporto Amerigo Vespucci** (www.aeroporto.firenze.it), is at Peretola, about 5km (3 miles) northwest of the city and is also known as Aeroporto Peretola. It handles domestic as well as a handful of European flights. From the UK, British Airways (www.britishairways.com) fly direct, daily, from London City Airport while Vueling (www.vueling.com) have some direct flights from Gatwick. Since 2019, Tramvia Line 2 has connected the airport with the city centre in just over 20 minutes.

Could you please take these bags to the bus/train/taxi, please? **Mi porti queste valige fino all'autobus/al treno/al taxi, per favore?**
What time does the train for Florence leave? **A che ora parte il treno per Firenze?**

Another option is to fly to Bologna's **G. Marconi Airport** (www.bologna-airport.it), 66km (41 miles) north of Florence. This route is served by British Airways, and these flights are often cheaper than on the Pisa route. Ryanair and easyJet also fly to Bologna from the UK. A shuttle bus operates between Bologna's airport and the centre of Bologna. Trains run about twice hourly and the journey to Florence takes just over an hour.

APPS

Free, useful apps for exploring the city include the **FeelFlorence app** (www.feelflorence.it), offering customizable itineraries. The **In Tuscany with Dante app** (www.santacroceopera.it) showcases places in and around Florence linked to the poet, launched in 2021 (commemorating 700 years since his death).

If intending to use the bus or tram systems, download the **Autolinee**

Toscane (www.at-bus.it) app, which covers ticketing for both.

For train travel to and from Florence's Santa Maria Novella station, save time and hassle at the on-site machines by using the excellent **Trenitalia app** (www.trenitalia.com).

International taxi apps such as Uber (www.uber.com) are available in Florence, but charge significantly higher rates than regular taxis, which can be hailed with the handy appTaxi app (https://apptaxi.it).

BICYCLE HIRE

Vehicles have been banned from the city centre in an effort to reduce congestion and pollution. Cycling is becoming increasingly popular among Florentines and there are a growing number of bike lanes. However, cyclists need their wits about them to steer a course through the hordes of tourists around the Duomo. Two highly rated bicycle rental outfits are found on Via San Zanobi: Florence By Bike (Via San Zanobi 54r; www.florencebybike.it) and Alinari (Via San Zanobi 38r; www.alinarirental.com).

BUDGETING FOR YOUR TRIP

The currency in Italy is the euro. For a rough guide as to how much things cost, the following is a list of average prices:

Drinks: Beer €2–4; glass of house wine €3–5; soft drinks €2–4. Waiter service will often cost twice as much as drinking at the bar.

Hotels: (Double room with bath, including tax and service, high-season rates): 5-star from €450, 4-star €250–450, 3-star €150–250, 2-star €120–150, 1-star under €120. Dorm beds start around €35.

Meals: Light lunch €20–25, three course dinner with wine in a good establishment €50 plus, coffee €1.50–4.

Museums: Admission fees range from approximately €2 for the small church museums to between €7 and €30 for some of the major collections. There are reductions for all visitors under-18 (ID required), while entrance is free for all EU citizens under-18 and over-65. The majority of the state museums are free to the public on the first Sunday of every month from October to March. If visiting several museums, a museum pass (see

Tourist Passes) can potentially offer savings.

Public transport: €1.70 for a single bus or tram ticket (valid for 90 minutes); €15.50 for a carnet of 10 tickets.

CAR HIRE (See also Driving)

Forget about driving in Florence. Cars are banned from the centre and must be left in the car parks on the edge of the city (https://fatturazione.fipark.com; most charge around €20/day). It's considerably cheaper to park a bit farther away at Villa Constanza (https://parcheggiovillacostanza.it), linked by tram to the centre (22min, leaving roughly every 5min), costing €2 for 1–4hr, €5 for 4–10hr and €7 for 10–24hr. Zones reading Zona Traffico Limitato (ZLT) mark the no-go areas.

If you decide to hire a car to tour Tuscany, prices begin around €300 a week for an economy car. In Florence, Via Borgo Ognissanti has a concentration of car-hire firms including **Budget** (Borgo Ognissanti 128r; www.budgetautonoleggio.it) and **TuscanybyCar** (Borgo Ognissanti 142r; www.tuscany-by-car.it). Cars can also be hired at Pisa and Florence airports. Booking from the UK is generally much cheaper than hiring on arrival. Most firms take and hold a credit card payment, which serves as the charge on return of the car. The minimum rental age varies from 19–25. Tuscany is well served by motorways though tolls are expensive.

I'd like to rent a car. **Vorrei noleggiare una macchina.**
…for one day/a week. …**per un giorno/una settimana.**
I want full insurance. **Voglio l'assicurazione completa.**

CLIMATE

Summer is often oppressively hot and sticky (the hills surrounding Florence capture the heat and humidity), while midwinter can be unpleasantly cold. The wettest months are October to April. The best times to visit are in spring and autumn, when temperatures are milder, but May and September have become extremely popular and crowded months to visit.

	J	F	M	A	M	J	J	A	S	O	N	D
°C												
max	11	13	16	19	24	28	31	31	27	21	15	11
min	2	3	5	8	12	15	18	18	14	10	5	3
°F												
max	52	55	60	65	75	82	89	89	80	70	58	52
min	36	37	41	46	53	59	64	64	58	50	41	37

CRIME AND SAFETY

Petty crime is a major problem in Florence, particularly pickpocketing and the snatching of handbags and jewellery, especially in crowded areas, busy markets and on public buses. You should take all the usual precautions against theft – do not carry large amounts of cash, leave your valuables in the hotel safe. Never leave your bags or valuables in view in a parked car; and never leave your bags in a car boot overnight, even if out of sight. The only real danger is from possible pickpockets, especially in crowded areas, busy markets and on public buses. If you have a shoulder bag, wear it across your body – it is harder to snatch.

Any theft or loss must be reported immediately to the police; make sure you obtain a copy of the report in order to comply with your travel insurance. If your passport is lost or stolen, inform your consulate immediately.

I want to report a theft. **Voglio denunciare un furto.**
My wallet/passport/ticket has been stolen. **Mi hanno rubato il portafoglio/il passaporto/il biglietto.**
I've lost my passport/wallet/bag/purse. **Ho perso il passaporto/il portafoglio/la borsa/la borsetta.**

DRIVING

Motorists planning to take their vehicle into Italy need a full driving licence, a Motor Insurance Certificate and a Vehicle Registration Document. Motorists must be over-18 to drive in Italy. If coming from the UK or Ireland, headlights must be adjusted for driving on the right and your number plate or a sticker must display the country that the car is registered in. The use of seatbelts in the front and back is obligatory; fines for non-compliance are stiff. A red warning triangle and reflective jackets must be carried in case of breakdown. Motorcycle riders must wear helmets. Documents must be carried at all times.

Driving conditions. Drive on the right, pass on the left. Give way to traffic coming from the right. Unless otherwise indicated speed limits in Italy are: 50kmh (30mph) in towns and built-up areas, 90kmh (55mph) on main roads and 130kmh (80mph) on highways.

Traffic police. *(Polizia stradale)*. Italian traffic police are authorised to impose on-the-spot fines for speeding and other traffic offences, such as driving while intoxicated (over 0.05 percent alcohol in your bloodstream) or stopping in a no-stopping zone. All cities, and many towns and villages, have signs posted on the outskirts indicating the telephone number of the local traffic police headquarters or *Carabinieri* (see Police). Police have recently become stricter about speeding.

Accidents and Breakdowns. Should you be involved in a road accident, dial **112** for the *carabinieri* (police). If your car is stolen or broken into, contact the Urban Police Headquarters *(Questura)* in Florence at Via Zara 2, and get a copy of their report for your insurance claim.

In the event of a breakdown dial **116**. This will put you in touch with the ACI (Automobile Club d'Italia), the national automobile organisation. About every 2km (1.5 miles or so) on the *autostrada* there's an emergency call box marked 'SOS'. Drivers of broken-down vehicles are required to warn other vehicles by placing a red triangular danger sign at least 50 metres (150ft) behind the vehicle. Reflective jackets should be worn.

Driving in Florence. Taking a car to Florence is not worth the hassle. The centre of Florence (within the circle of avenues or *viali* that surround it on both sides of the River Arno) is a restricted ZTL area (*zona traffico limitato* – limited traffic zone). Between 7.30am and 8pm Monday–Friday and 7.30am and 4pm Saturday, only residents with special permits on their windscreens are allowed into this zone. CCTV cameras are placed at entrance points. If you need access to enter to offload baggage and passengers inform your hotel in advance of the registration number. This will be forwarded electronically to the relevant office. You must then go and park outside the ZTL. Motorist fines are very heavy and vehicles are frequently towed away.

Curva pericolosa Dangerous bend/curve
Deviazione Detour
Divieto di sorpasso No passing
Divieto di sosta No stopping
Lavori in corso Roadworks/Men working
Pericolo Danger
Rallentare Slow down
Senso vietato/unico No entry/One-way street
Vietato l'ingresso No entry
Zona pedonale Pedestrian zone

ELECTRICITY

220V/50Hz AC is standard in Italy. An adaptor *(una presa complementare)* for Continental-style sockets will be needed; American 110V appliances also require a transformer.

EMBASSIES AND CONSULATES

In Florence:

US (consulate): Lungarno Vespucci 38, tel: 055-266 951, https://it.usembassy.gov/it.

In Rome:

Australia (embassy): Via Antonio Bosio 5, tel: 06-852 721, http://italy.embassy.gov.au.

Canada (embassy): Via Zara 30, tel: 06-854 441, www.canadainternational.gc.ca.

New Zealand (embassy): Via Clitunno 44, tel: 06-853 7501.

Republic of Ireland (embassy): Via Giacomo Medici 1, tel: 06-585 2381, www.dfa.ie/irish-embassy/italy.

UK (embassy): Via XX Settembre 80a, tel: 06-4220 0001, www.gov.uk/government/world/organisations/british-embassy-rome.

US (embassy): Via Vittorio Veneto 121, tel: 06-46741, http://it.usembassy.gov.

EMERGENCIES

If you don't speak Italian, find a local resident to help you or talk to the English-speaking operator on the telephone assisted service, tel: **170**.

Police **112**

General emergency **113**

Fire **115**

Paramedics **118**

Please, can you place an emergency call to the…? **Per favore, può fare una telefonata d'emergenza…?**

police **alla polizia**

fire brigade **ai pompieri**

hospital **all'ospedale**

GETTING THERE

By air. From the UK and US, there are scheduled flights from the major cities to the international gateway airports of Rome and Milan, where you can catch a connecting flight to Pisa (80km/50 miles from Florence) or to Florence itself. Non-stop flights from the UK connect London with Pisa, Florence and Bologna. British Airways, (www.britishairways.com), from London City airport and Vueling, (www.vueling.com), from Gatwick to Florence. Ryanair, (www.ryanair.com), offers low-cost, direct flights from London Stansted to Pisa and Bologna 100km (60 miles) from Florence. British Airways and easyJet (www.easyjet.com) also fly to Pisa and Bologna.

By rail. Florence's Stazione Santa Maria Novella Station is well connected to Milan, Bologna, Turin and Rome. While journeying by rail from north of the Alps isn't as cheap as arriving on a budget airline, it can be well worthwhile – not least for the wonderful scenery – depending on the time, number and length of transfers required. From London (St Pancras), travel to Paris (Gare du Nord) on Eurostar (www.eurostar.com), then board a high-speed Frecciarossa (www.trenitalia.com) or TGV (www.sncf-connect.com) train from Paris to Turin or Milan to connect to Florence. Italian State Railways (www.trenitalia.com) offer fare reductions in certain cases. These are subject to variation, but there are almost always discounts for children and groups available. Ask at any railway station or go to the website for current information. These tickets can be purchased at home or in Italy.

GUIDES AND TOURS

For art and history tours contact the Florence Tour Guides Association (https://guidefirenzeagt.it), Florence's official tourism office (www.feelflorence.it) or ArtViva (www.artviva.com).

Some travel agencies and bus companies offer organised bus tours of the countryside around Florence, including excursions to San Gimignano/Siena or Pisa. Details can be obtained through your hotel, tourist information offices and local travel agencies.

We'd like an English-speaking guide. **Desideriamo una guida che parla inglese.**
I need an English interpreter. **Ho bisogno di un interprete d'inglese.**

HEALTH AND MEDICAL CARE

(see also Emergencies)

EU residents. EU citizens are entitled to the same medical treatment as Italian citizens. Visitors will need to have a **European Health Insurance Card** (EHIC, www.nhs.uk) before they go.

UK citizens: Italy and the UK have a reciprocal agreement regarding hospital treatment. UK citizens should obtain a UK-issued **Global Health**

Insurance Card (GHIC, www.nhs.uk) before travelling. This entitles them to low-cost and sometimes free medical treatment. Full travel insurance, however, is still advised.

For US and Canadian citizens: Canadian citizens are covered by a reciprocal arrangement between the Italian and Canadian governments, but US citizens are strongly advised to take out private health insurance. Remember to keep receipts as a record in case you need to show evidence of your medical treatment at a later stage.

I need a doctor/dentist. **Ho bisogno di un medico/dentista.**
It hurts here. **Ho un dolore qui.**
a stomachache **un mal di stomaco**
a fever **la febbre**
sunburn/sunstroke **una scottatura di sole/un colpo di sole**

Medical emergencies: There is an accident and emergency department in the city centre at Ospedale Santa Maria Nuova, Piazza Santa Maria Nuova, tel: 055-69381.

Pharmacies: Most pharmacies *(farmacie)* follow retail hours; the one in the Santa Maria Novella railway station stays open all night. In Italy, pharmacists are able to diagnose and prescribe mild medication for which, elsewhere, you would normally need a prescription. If it is not a true emergency, make a visit to a pharmacist instead of the hospital.

LANGUAGE

English is widely spoken in Florence, especially by the young, and you can get by without a word of Italian. However, it is well worth the effort in Florence – birthplace of modern Italian – to know at least a few phrases.

Local people will welcome and encourage any attempt you make to use their language. When you enter a shop, restaurant or office, the greeting is always *buon giorno* (good morning) or *buona sera* (good afternoon/evening – used from around 1pm onwards). When enquiring, start with *per favore* (please), and for any service rendered say *grazie* (thanks), to which the reply is *prego* (don't mention it, you're welcome). Accompany a handshake with *piacere* (it's a pleasure). A more familiar greeting, used among friends, is *ciao*, which means both 'Hi' and 'See you later'.

LGBTQ+ TRAVEL

Florence is an easy-going destination for LGBTQ+ visitors, with a lively local scene. The national gay rights organisation, Arcigay (www.arcigay.it), has an active branch here (Via Enrico Forlanini 164) that can provide help and information. Another useful resource is www.gayfriendlyitaly.com. Of Florence's few gay bars, Piccolo (Borgo Santa Croce 23r; www.instagram.com/piccolo_94) is a favourite, situated on a side street just south of Piazza Santa Croce.

I'd like a street plan of... **Vorrei una pianta della città...**
I'd like a road map of this region. **Vorrei una carta stradale di questa regione.**

MONEY

Currency. The official currency used in Italy is the euro (€). Notes are in denominations of 5, 10, 20, 50, 100, 200 and 500 euros; coins in 1 and 2 euros and 1, 2, 5, 10, 20 and 50 cents.

Banks and currency exchange offices. Changing money in a bank can be time-consuming and opening hours are limited but they generally offer the best rates. Exchange offices, open all day and at weekends, can be found all over Florence, and at the railway station. Passports are usually required when changing money. If intending to make large withdrawals, alert your bank at home in advance that you will be using your card.

ATMs and credit cards. Automatic currency-exchange machines *(bancomat)* are operated by most banks and can also be found in the centre of town. Most hotels, shops and restaurants take credit cards, increasingly via contactless payment.

I want to change some pounds/dollars. **Desidero cambiare delle sterline/dei dollari.**
Can I pay with this credit card? **Posso pagare con la carta di credito?**
Where is the bank/atm? **Dov'è il banco/bancomat?**

OPENING HOURS

Banks. These are usually open Monday–Friday 8.30am–1.30pm and 2.30–4pm.

Churches. Generally closed for sightseeing at lunchtime, approximately noon–3pm or even later. Touristic (non-devotional) visits are strongly discouraged during Sunday morning services.

Museums and art galleries. Opening hours of museums and art galleries vary hugely and some change their hours from season to season. They are generally open from 8.15/9am–4.30pm, or in the case of some of the main sights, 6.30pm. Closing day is usually Monday (including for the Galleria dell'Accademia and Uffizi), though some places close on Tuesday (including the Bargello and Medici Chapels). If Monday is a holiday, some museums and galleries close the following day. Some sights have restricted opening hours at weekends, especially Sundays. Find an exhaustive, updated list of opening hours at the tourist bureau's website (www.feelflorence.it).

Shops. Although many of the large shops and supermarkets now remain open all day *(no-stop or orario continuato)*, the majority still adhere to the decades-old Florentine tradition of closing for a long lunch and on Monday mornings (Wednesday afternoons for food shops). Generally, shop opening hours are: Monday 3.30/4–7.30/8pm and Tuesday–Saturday 8.30/9am–1/1.30pm and 3.30/4pm–7/8pm. Food shops tend to open earlier than this and close earlier, while clothes shops may do the opposite, often not opening until 10am. Some of the central Florentine shops remain open for some part of Sunday, but many still close on that day. Some shops close for August or at least for part of it and if you see a sign that says *chiuso per ferie* with dates, it indicates they are closed for a holiday and usually indicates the date when they will reopen.

POLICE

Florence's city police, the Vigili Urbani, handle traffic and parking and perform other routine tasks. While the officers rarely speak English, they are courteous and helpful towards tourists. The *carabinieri*, a paramilitary force, wear light-brown or blue uniforms with peaked caps, and deal with more serious crimes and demonstrations. Outside town, the Polizia Stradale patrol the highways, issue speeding tickets and assist with breakdowns (see Driving).

Police Headquarters *(Questura)* and Stolen Vehicles Department, Via Zara 2, tel: 055-49771.

Carabinieri Regional Headquarters (the only station where you're likely to find someone who speaks English): Borgo Ognissanti 48, tel: 055-27661.

Polizia Stradale (Traffic Police), tel: 055-50681.

Polizia Assistenza Turistica (Tourist Police), Via Pietrapiana 50r, tel: 055-203 911.

Where's the nearest police station? **Dov'è il più vicino punto di polizia?**

Where's the nearest post office? **Dov'è l'ufficio postale più vicino?**

Have you received any mail for…? **C'è posta per…?**

I'd like a stamp for this letter/postcard. **Desidero un francobollo per questa lettera/cartolina.**

PUBLIC HOLIDAYS

Banks, offices, government institutions, most shops and many museums are closed on national holidays, as well as on the Florentines' local holiday on 24 June, commemorating the town's patron saint, San Giovanni Battista (St John the Baptist). During the long weekend of 15 August, almost everything in Florence (and Italy) closes.

1 January *Capodanno/Primo dell'Anno* New Year's Day

6 January *Epifania* Epiphany
25 April *Festa della Liberazione* Liberation Day
1 May *Festa del Lavoro* Labour Day
2 June *Festa della Repubblica* (Republic Day)
24 June *Fest di San Giovanni* Patron Saint of Florence
15 August *Ferragosto* Feast of the Assumption
1 November *Ognissanti* All Saints' Day
8 December *Concezione Immacolata* Immaculate Conception
25 December *Natale* Christmas Day
26 December *Santo Stefano* St Stephen's Day
Movable dates:
Pasqua Easter
Pasquetta/Lunedì di Pasqua Easter Monday

RELIGION

Italy is an overwhelmingly Catholic country, and the ideals and influence of the Vatican permeate Italian life and politics. Mass is celebrated in English in the Duomo (every Saturday at 5pm), in the Church of St James (American Episcopal, Via Bernardo Rucellai 9, Sundays at 9am and 11am) and at St Mark's English Church (Via Maggio, 18, on Sundays at 10.30am). In churches, shorts, miniskirts or bare shoulders are not considered respectable.

TELEPHONES

The country code for Italy is **39**, and the area code for the city of Florence is **055**. Note that you must dial the 055 prefix even when making local calls within the city of Florence. When calling from abroad you retain the initial zero on the local code. To make an international call from Italy, dial 00, followed by the country code (**44** for the UK, **1** for US and Canada, **61** for Australia, **353** for Ireland and **64** for New Zealand), then the area code and number.

Mobile phones. Mobile phone use in EU countries may be included in your plan for no extra cost but to be sure check with your network provider for information on roaming costs before visiting. If you intend to stay for long, consider installing an Italian SIM card, available from any mobile phone shop. Alternatively, if compatible with your phone, consider a digital eSIM instead of a physical card.

Give me coins/a telephone card, please. **Per favore, mi dia monette/una scheda telefonica.**

TIME DIFFERENCES

Italian time coincides with most of Western Europe – Greenwich Mean Time plus one hour. In summer, an hour is added for Daylight Saving Time.

New York	London	**Florence**	Jo'burg	Sydney
6am	11am	**noon**	1pm	8pm

TIPPING

Many restaurants in Florence levy a *coperto* or cover charge and/or a service charge so tipping is not necessarily expected. If you want to give a tip, leave 10 percent in a restaurant and small change at a bar.

It is also customary to tip bellboys, doormen and lavatory attendants for their service. Taxi drivers do not expect a full 10 percent, and normal practice by Italians is simply to round up the fare.

Thank you, this is for you. **Grazie, questo è per Lei.**
Keep the change. **Tenga il resto.**

TOILETS

You will find public toilets in airports, railway and bus stations, museums and art galleries. The men's may be indicated by *'signori'*, the ladies' by *'signore'*. All bars have toilet facilities, but buy a drink out of courtesy before you use them.

Where are the toilets? **Dove sono i gabinetti?**

TOURIST INFORMATION

In Florence the Agenzia per il Turismo di Firenze (www.feelflorence.it), the city's official tourism office, comprises the most up-to-date and exhaustive resource for tourism information, with English-speaking staff, free maps, reams of information on sights and even a handy app. The tourist office is at Piazza della Stazione 4 (Mon–Sat 9am–7pm; Sun 9am–5.30pm), sharing the entrance to Santa Maria Novella, just opposite the main train station. Additional infopoints (Mon–Sat 9am–7pm; Sun 9am–2pm) are at Via Cavour 1r, north of the Duomo; Borgo Santa Croce 29r, south of Piazza di Santa Croce; and Florence Airport.

Fiesole: Via Portigiani 3, (www.fiesoleforyou.it; usually daily 10am–1pm and 2–6pm, but opening times vary so check the website).

Pisa: Piazza del Duomo 7 (www.turismo.pisa.it; usually daily 9.30am–7.30pm; check website).

San Gimignano: Piazza del Duomo 1 (www.sangimignano.com; Mar–Oct daily 10am–1pm and 3–7pm; Nov–Feb 10am–1pm and 2–6pm).

Siena: Piazza del Campo 1 (www.terredisiena.it; daily 9am–6pm).

TOURIST PASSES

Depending on the aims of your visit, you can choose from a number of tourist passes to save time and money. Note that at certain popular attractions, time slot reservations are advisable (particularly for the Uffizi) and in certain cases required (among these Brunelleschi's dome and Brancacci Chapel).

For €85, the **Firenze Card** (https://firenzecard.it) offers good value for those planning on museum hopping over several days. Valid for 72 hours, it grants entry to more than 60 museums, galleries and other sites including the Accademia, Uffizi, Palazzo Vecchio, Medici Chapels and the Santa Croce complex. Though far less exhaustive, the **Florence Pass** (€115; www.florence-pass-digital.com) covers the city's top attractions: a climb to either the Duomo's bell tower or dome plus admission to the

Uffizi and Accademia galleries. Alternatively, to cover all of the Duomo's attractions, the Opera di Santa Maria del Fiore (https://duomo.firenze.it) offers a **Piazza del Duomo** pass, available in three tiers: the **Brunelleschi Pass** (€30 includes access to the dome, bell tower, baptistery, crypt and the Opera del Duomo Museum; the **Giotto Pass**; €20) excludes the dome while the **Ghiberti Pass** (€15) excludes both the dome and the bell tower.

TRANSPORT

The centre of Florence is small enough to cover on foot. If you want to cross the town by public transport there are fast and efficient electric buses (C1, C2 and C3) stopping near the main sights. A pair of tram lines conveniently links the centre to the airport and Villa Constanza (for inter-city buses).

Buses and trams. Ticketing for both bus and tramway transport in Florence is operated by **Autolinee Toscane** (www.at-bus.it). In 2024, onboard contactless payment was rolled out on all buses and trams. Alternatively, download the AT app to purchase, activate and display tickets on your phone. Tangible tickets can still be bought from tobacconists *(tabacchi)*, newsstands, bars or automatic ticket machines at main points throughout the city. Tickets are €1.70 for a 90-minute journey or €15.50 for a carnet of 10 tickets. Paper tickets must be stamped in the appropriate machines on board the bus at the beginning of the journey. Officials periodically conduct spot checks, imposing stiff fines – no excuses accepted.

The **Tramvia network** has two useful lines linking the central hub of Alamanni (at Santa Maria Novella) to the suburbs. Opened in 2010, Line 1 connects Villa Costanza (departure point for long-haul buses) to the southwest of the city. Opened in 2019, Line 2 links Peretola (Florence) Airport. Expansions to Line 2 (plus two other lines) remain in the works.

Inter-city buses: Autolinee Toscane (www.at-bus.it) has regular connections from Florence to Siena and Lucca. For Siena (1hr 30min), take Line 131 from Santa Maria Novella's bus station. For Lucca (1hr), take DD Line from tram Line 2's Guidoni stop (just before the airport stop). Alternatively, there are sporadic inter-city services run by bus companies like Itabus (www.itabus.it) and Flixbus (www.flixbus.co.uk; tel: 055-204 111).

Taxis. Taxis are white and can be picked up at ranks in the main city squares, or called by telephone (tel: 055-4390 or 055-4242) or app (https://apptaxi.it) but not hailed. There are fixed rates from the airport to the centre.

Trains. The Italian State Railway, FS (Ferrovie dello Stato; www.trenitalia.com) has an excellent rail network. There are regular services to Rome, Milan, Venice (to name but a few) and other European cities, plus fast services to Tuscan cities such as Arezzo and Pisa.

When's the next bus/ train to…? **Quando parte il prossimo autobus/treno per…?**
single (one-way) **andata**
return (round-trip) **andata e ritorno**
first/second class **prima/seconda classe**
What's the fare to…? **Qual'è la tariffa per…?**
I'd like to make a seat reservation. **Vorrei prenotare un posto.**

VISA AND ENTRY REQUIREMENTS

Visa-free entry. For citizens of the UK, US, Australia, Canada and New Zealand, among other countries (see www.esteri.it), a valid passport is required for stays of up to 90 days within a 180-day period in the Schengen Area.

Visas. For stays of more than 90 days, a visa *(permesso di soggiorno)* or residence permit is required. Regulations may change, so check with the Italian Embassy (www.esteri.it) or in your home country before you travel.

Customs. Free exchange of non-duty-free goods for personal use is allowed between countries within the European Union (EU). Refer to your home country's regulating organisation for a current list of import restrictions.

Currency restrictions. A customs declaration is required to bring €10,000 cash (or equivalent in currency) into or out of the country.

I've nothing to declare. **Non ho niente da dichiarare.**
It's for my personal use. **È per mio uso personale.**

Index

THE **MINI** ROUGH GUIDE TO **FLORENCE**

First Edition 2025

Editor: Lizzie Horrocks
Author: Anthon Jackson
Picture Editor: Piotr Kala
Picture Manager: Tom Smyth
Cartography Update: Katie Bennett
Layout: Ankur Guha
Production Operations Manager: Katie Bennett
Publishing Technology Manager: Rebeka Davies
Head of Publishing: Sarah Clark
Photography Credits: iStock 8, 13C, 21, 22, 37, 39, 41, 43, 44, 70, 84, 86, 89, 102; Public domain 29, 31, 32, 48; Shutterstock 1, 4, 5, 7, 11, 12C, 12C, 12TC, 12CL, 12TL, 12TL, 13, 13T, 13C, 14TL, 14CL, 14CR, 14B, 16TL, 16CL, 16CR, 16B, 18TL, 18CL, 18CR, 18B, 20, 25, 26, 34, 47, 51, 53, 54, 55, 57, 60, 62, 64, 66, 68, 72, 73, 75, 77, 79, 80, 83, 94, 96, 99, 101, 104, 107, 108, 110, 112, 114; Steve McDonald/Apa Publications 59, 92
Cover Credits: Duomo di Firenze **Shutterstock**

About the author
Anthon Jackson is an American, Denmark-based writer and photographer. He has contributed to more than 25 travel books for Rough Guides and other series. Follow Anthon on Instagram @anthonjackson_, on X @janthonjackson, and visit his website, anthonjackson.com.

Distribution
UK, Ireland and Europe: Apa Publications (UK) Ltd; sales@roughguides.com
United States and Canada: Ingram Publisher Services; ips@ingramcontent.com
Australia and New Zealand: Booktopia; retailer@booktopia.com.au
Worldwide: Apa Publications (UK) Ltd; sales@roughguides.com

Special Sales, Content Licensing and CoPublishing
Rough Guides can be purchased in bulk quantities at discounted prices. We can create special editions, personalised jackets and corporate imprints tailored to your needs. sales@roughguides.com; http://roughguides.com

Printed in Czech Republic

This book was produced using **Typefi** automated publishing software.

Contact us
Every effort has been made to provide accurate information in this publication, but changes are inevitable. The publisher cannot be held responsible for any resulting loss, inconvenience or injury sustained by any traveller as a result of information or advice contained in the guide. We would appreciate it if readers would call our attention to any errors or outdated information, or if you feel we've left something out. Please send your comments with the subject line "Rough Guide Mini Florence Update" to mail@uk.roughguides.com.